Set design by Mark Wendland

Photo by Russell Caldwell

A scene from the La Jolla Playhouse production of *Sheridan*.

SHERIDAN

OR, SCHOOLED IN SCANDAL

BY DAVID GRIMM

DRAMATISTS
PLAY SERVICE
INC.

ACKNOWLEDGMENTS

I would like to extend my deepest thanks to Morgan Jenness (artists' representative, dramaturg, and friend), Mark Brokaw (the sort of director playwrights dream about), and Eleanor Holdridge (who originally suggested the idea for this play) for their encouragement, support, and belief in this project. I would also like to thank Paul Zablocki, Tina Ball, Dick Beebe, Beth Blickers, Jane Cullinan, Rachel Davidson, Annie Hamburger, Patrick Herold, Diana and Honour Kane, Neel Keller, David Mooney, John Santoianni, and all the actors who took part in readings and workshops over the years (with a special remembrance to Bill Duff-Griffin).

Thank you.

AUTHOR'S NOTE

This is a work of fiction. It is not intended to be a history lesson, a biography, or a truthful account of events from the past. It is inspired by a letter written by Lord Byron in which he discussed his admiration for the aging Richard Brinsley Sheridan who had long since given up writing for the theatre and had become an old drunk, barely able to hold on to his seat in the House of Commons. From this small detail I have spun a tale about friendship, loyalty, betrayal, personal morality, and the integrity of the artist. In doing so, I have taken great liberty with historical fact and make no apology for it.

The other major inspiration for the play was the embarrassing attempt by the United States government to define artistic expression which resulted in the defunding of the National Endowment for the Arts. This is a play about a society that believes it has the right to peer into people's bedrooms and decide what is decent and what is not; a society that thrives on intrigue, political scandal and moral indignation; a society that has lost all sense of its own civility. It is about England in the late eighteenth century; it is about America in the early twenty-first century.

A word or two about performance style: while the humorous elements of the play — King George, for example — reach an almost slapstick dimension, they should never be played merely for laughs. The humor is borne out of confusion, anger, pain. Never lose track of the emotional truth lurking behind the clownish mask. Sheridan himself is a master dissembler, hiding his hurt behind a jest. He deflects and tries to escape with his jokes, but the pain is ever present.

One last note: the text printed here is a revision of the play that premiered at the La Jolla Playhouse in the summer of 2000. Two characters (Eliza and Fitzherbert) have been eliminated and some reshaping has taken place.

SHERIDAN OR, SCHOOLED IN SCANDAL was originally produced by the La Jolla Playhouse (Annie Hamburger, Artistic Director; Terrence Dwyer, Managing Director; Neel Keller, Artistic Associate) in San Diego, California, on July 18, 2000. It was directed by Mark Brokaw; the set design was by Mark Wendland; the lighting design was by Mark McCullough; the sound design was by John Gromada; the costume design was by Annie Smart; the dramaturg was Elizabeth Bennett; the stage manager was Dan da Silva; and the assistant stage manager was Joyce Davidson. The cast was as follows:

BYRON	Jeremy Shamos
DEVONSHIRE	Sandra Shipley
HOPKINS	Christopher Burris
SHERIDAN	Sherman Howard
PERDITA	Francesca Faridany
POPE	Bairbre Dowling
FOX	Robert Machray
PITT	Charles Janasz
CREWE	Maria Dizzia
GEORGE III	Ray Reinhardt
PRINNIE	Trey Lyford
FITZHERBERT *	Alison Weller
ELIZA *	Francesca Faridany
RAMMAGE	Ray Reinhardt
McKEYE	Robert Machray

* These roles were cut subsequent to the La Jolla Playhouse production.

5

CHARACTERS

LORD BYRON, a young poet

DUCHESS OF DEVONSHIRE, a titled lady

HOPKINS, a stage manager

RICHARD BRINSLEY SHERIDAN, a playwright

PERDITA ROBINSON, an actress

MISS POPE, an actress

CHARLES JAMES FOX, a member of Parliament

WILLIAM PITT, Prime Minister

GEORGE III, King of England

MRS. CREWE, a widow
(played by the actor playing Miss Pope)

PRINNIE, Prince of Wales
(played by the actor playing Hopkins)

FATHER RAMMAGE, a priest
(played by the actor playing George III)

JUSTICE McKEYE, a judge
(played by the actor playing Fox)

PLACE

London.

TIME

The end of the eighteenth century.

6

SHERIDAN

OR, SCHOOLED IN SCANDAL

ACT ONE

Scene 1

A terrace off the Duchess of Devonshire's apartments. Late afternoon sun. The sounds of stringed instruments mixed with the whispered chatter of women and the fluttering of fans from the next room. A man in his early twenties, dressed recklessly. His hair is wild. He walks with a limp: Byron.

BYRON. London. Back in time for autumn. In time to entertain the rich and illiterate in their own homes. Bottles of port. Forced smiles. The latest fashion. Numbing. The smell of winter coming. Sunsets get sadder and more elegant. Still, darkness. Candles. Dust. *(Pause; he breathes.)* Yet another literary salon. *(The Duchess of Devonshire appears with a drink. A very well-dressed woman of a certain age. Elegant. Cultured.)*

DEVONSHIRE. Lord Byron, you're alone. We thought you'd left us.

BYRON. I needed to take the air.

DEVONSHIRE. We found your poem ... invigorating.

BYRON. A few of the ladies looked faint. I thought they'd shit themselves.

DEVONSHIRE. We are not accustomed to your sort of —

BYRON. Honesty?

DEVONSHIRE. Confrontation. Pity you're not published. Print has a way of making men seem almost respectable. May I offer you ·

a drink? *(Byron is served a drink.)* Three years in Turkey and Greece have done much for you.

BYRON. Three years have done little for London society. It's as small-minded as ever.

DEVONSHIRE. I must admit, I have never been particularly fond of poetry. This need for metaphor — frankly, it's tiresome. However, it is fashionable these days to admire a well-turned verse or a capering couplet and, being a woman of mode, I must embrace the current style. I have never cared much for men, either. But I do appreciate what they represent. Tell me, what does a young man such as yourself aspire to most?

BYRON. What any young man aspires to. Fortune, fame, fornication. Do I shock you?

DEVONSHIRE. I am far too rich to be shocked. In fact, I can place these aspirations within your reach. I can hand you your dreams like a bottle of port and you can drink all you like.

BYRON. The profit of dreams is best earned and not purchased, Your Grace. What is the Duchess of Devonshire after?

DEVONSHIRE. Power. That is what men represent. I would like to publish one of your poems. The one you read tonight. It's very new.

BYRON. The latest fashion?

DEVONSHIRE. Lord Byron, let me be blunt. I did not invite you to my home solely to recite your little masterpiece. I invited you to discuss a business transaction.

BYRON. Serving up my poems in today's conservative climate doesn't show very sound business sense. I fail to see the point.

DEVONSHIRE. You will. Tell me, how well do you know Mister Sheridan?

BYRON. Richard Brinsley Sheridan? The man is only our greatest living writer for the stage and a highly respected member of Parliament.

DEVONSHIRE. I did not ask for his credentials, but I ask if you do know him.

BYRON. *The Rivals* — *School for Scandal* — I've read and witnessed every play he ever wrote. The man's a genius.

DEVONSHIRE. Be that as it may, this genius has involved himself in a very dangerous enterprise. His theatre, the Drury Lane, has fallen upon hard times. In attempting to maintain its solvency, he has turned to the Prince of Wales for financial support.

BYRON. There is nothing dangerous about royal patronage.

DEVONSHIRE. In exchange for these moneys, Mister Sheridan has been arranging assignations for the prince. He has procured for him a Mrs. Maria Fitzherbert — a woman of low birth. An army widow. And a Catholic.

BYRON. I have no interest in malicious gossip, Your Grace. If you'll excuse me —

DEVONSHIRE. The prince has, for lack of better words, fallen in love with the woman. Sheridan has been transporting their letters. Acting as their secret messenger.

BYRON. The private dealings between discreet persons are of no concern to me or anyone.

DEVONSHIRE. Ah, but you're wrong. The private is political, Lord Byron. And the future of our royal house cannot be toyed with by the likes of Mister Sheridan. Such an affair cannot be allowed to continue.

BYRON. What is this matter to me?

DEVONSHIRE. I want you to intercept their letters.

BYRON. *(Pause; laughing.)* You hold the most intriguing salons, Your Grace. I bid you a good night.

DEVONSHIRE. Greece is a fascinating country, is it not? The people are so eager to oblige foreign citizens. I've heard stories. Some of which defy morality.

BYRON. I don't give a fig for morality. It is only envy thinly disguised.

DEVONSHIRE. I take it then you don't approve of Mister Pitt's committee.

BYRON. The ethics thing? Paying off mothers to turn in their sons for playing with themselves in the dark? It's primitive, barbaric and, as with all things that smack of the Middle Ages, typically English.

DEVONSHIRE. No, I suppose someone whose name has been linked in rumor to stable boys and farmhands would not approve of Mister Pitt's committee.

BYRON. *(Silence; uneasily:)* Again: gossip.

DEVONSHIRE. From very reliable sources.

BYRON. There's no proof to what you say.

DEVONSHIRE. Proof, my Lord Byron, is a thing of the past. I need only speak the word and link your name to it in the morning, you'd be hanging disgraced in the pillory by nightfall. The power of the word is a formidable one. I see why you poets are drawn to it. Today, it is not so important that a thing is true, but that it is said to be true. That is the glory of our modern age.

BYRON. There are laws which govern such slander, Your Grace.

DEVONSHIRE. Then pursue them in the courts if you can stand the risk.

BYRON. How dare you? This is an outrage!

DEVONSHIRE. *Au contraire.* This is business. Get me those letters and the Committee on Public Ethics needs never know of your little indiscretions.

BYRON. Why are you doing this? It's absurd! I've never even met Mister Sheridan!

DEVONSHIRE. You are a writer. You speak his language. I know you will not refuse me.

BYRON. No — I will not involve myself in your seedy little plots! This is no more than bitterness brought on by your disgrace at being passed up for the royal position yourself.

DEVONSHIRE. It is true I have been usurped. The prince forgets that my family, wealth, and title offer more than this common Catholic widow ever could. He also forgets that I am the sort of person who always has the last word. That is what has made me a success. That is why I will not bend. I don't expect a man to understand, but time is a woman's chiefest enemy. Her position in society depends on two things: youth and a good marriage. I have lost the one, I will not lose the other.

BYRON. I will not be the hobbyhorse on which you ride your way to court.

DEVONSHIRE. Oh, but you will.

BYRON. You would drag me through the mud all for a letter?

DEVONSHIRE. My dear Lord Byron, lives have been lost for less. I do so hope you make the right decision. After all, I would very much like to publish — what was it again? *Childe Harold's* something-or-other? I will leave you to consider all your options. *(She turns to go. Stops.)* Oh, and by the by — welcome back to England.

Scene 2

In the darkness —

PERDITA. *(Off.)* Give them back! Stop that! Come back here! *(Lights rise on the changing room of the Drury Lane Theatre. Early evening. A long table covered with a tablecloth. A jumble of papers, waistcoats, dresses, plates of food. Hopkins, a working-class boy of seventeen, is laying out props and organizing. Sheridan enters running. His wig is frazzled, his clothes are food-stained, and the top of his trousers is undone. He holds a bottle in one hand and a woman's undergarment in the other.)*
HOPKINS. Miss Pope is looking for you, sir. She's asking to be paid. *(Sheridan tosses the undergarment at Hopkins, belches loudly, then puts a finger to his lips to signal silence. He leaps under the table, hiding.)*
PERDITA. *(Off.)* You scoundrel! Give me back my — *(Hopkins stuffs the undergarment into his pocket as Perdita Robinson enters running, her dress undone, her hair wild.)* Hopkins, have you seen Sir pass through here in the last few minutes? *(Hopkins opens his mouth to respond when Sheridan shoots him a look from beneath the table. Hopkins shrugs. Perdita grumbles and exits running, closely avoiding Miss Pope, who enters eating from a plate of chicken.)*
MISS POPE. Hey-up — mind how you go! Well, boy? Where is he?
HOPKINS. I — well — he — who?
MISS POPE. I want my money! You tell that chiseling skinflint that my patience is at an end and I want my sodding pay! Have you done mending my wig?
HOPKINS. Yes, Miss Pope. I'll have it down directly. *(Perdita re-enters running.)*
PERDITA. What o'clock is it, Hopkins?
HOPKINS. Half hour to curtain, Miss Robinson.
PERDITA. Damn, damn, damn. *(Hopkins and Perdita exit running in separate directions. Miss Pope sits, props up a small mirror,*

11

and continues to eat as she applies her stage makeup.)
MISS POPE. Tut — it's disgraceful. I'm used like a workhorse round here. No consideration or respect. A man of his position, he ought to know better. *(Hopkins reenters with a red wig.)*
HOPKINS. Your wig, Miss Pope. *(Perdita has entered, disheartened. She sits and starts to apply her own makeup. She opens a newspaper before her.)*
PERDITA. He's nowhere to be found!
HOPKINS. Don't forget to take the pins out.
MISS POPE. If I'd seen him, you can be sure I'd give him a piece of my mind.
PERDITA. *(Sotto voce.)* If you think you can spare it, Miss Pope.
MISS POPE. And you, my dear — don't think you're on to anything new. Oldest story in the book. Oh yes, I once had looks. Heads and pockets turned for me —
PERDITA. *(Sotto voce.)* Stomachs too.
MISS POPE. Everyone's got something to sell. Though in my day you had to have talent as well as looks to get by.
PERDITA. And what you got now?
MISS POPE. Alas, at my age, they call it perseverance. *(Perdita feels something under the table. Stiffens.)* Of course, things'd be different if his wife were still alive. New dresses every other month, we had. Not like these days with the sorry old rags as last year, and those left over from the year before. *(Perdita straightens and gasps.)* But it's true! Wearing these tatters, it's no wonder his *School for Scandal* looks like a knocking-shop in a leper colony. *(Perdita flinches and stifles a giggle.)* Do you mock me, girl?
HOPKINS. I'm sure if we took down the hem and tacked on some tulle —
MISS POPE. Look at her! Snickering up her sleeve like a bloody monkey. Well I'm not staying here to be laughed at by a mealy-mouthed scrubber like her. Hopkins — come! *(Miss Pope exits, Hopkins rushing after her.)*
PERDITA. You shit-staring old cow! Why, I'll — *(Perdita rises after her, but falls and is instantly pulled under the table. She struggles out with Sheridan on top of her, kissing her neck and breasts.)* No! Mister Sheridan, stop! It's half hour to curtain!
SHERIDAN. Call me Dick.

PERDITA. What have you done with my pantalettes?

SHERIDAN. You smell good — like you've washed.

PERDITA. Stop it! A man of your age —

SHERIDAN. *(Feeling her breasts.)* This body!

PERDITA. — Like a dog in heat.

SHERIDAN. — Like jelly in a sling. *(During the following, he kisses her breasts and the rest of her body, working his way down.)*

PERDITA. You don't deserve me.

SHERIDAN. It is your generosity I am relying on. You help me to forget.

PERDITA. Six months ago you said you'd write me a play. I haven't seen a word on paper since.

SHERIDAN. Perdita, a promise is the most divine pledge. Don't debase it by holding me to it. You know I gave up writing with puberty.

PERDITA. What about all the poems you used to write your wife?

SHERIDAN. Love can play havoc with a man's senses.

PERDITA. Meaning you don't love me? How am I supposed to respect you?

SHERIDAN. *(Parting her legs.)* I don't want your respect. I want your body.

PERDITA. I am not a prostitute.

SHERIDAN. Then why do you insist on payment? *(She tightens her thighs around him in a scissor-hold and he cries out. She releases him and goes to the table where she sits and opens the newspaper.)* Oh, my back! I think you've crippled me. Come back here.

PERDITA. I want a man I can look up to, Richard. Someone I can be proud of. I once thought you were such a man. A soul of integrity, philosophy, ideals. A man who'd stand for something.

SHERIDAN. I'm standing for you right now, if you'd only have a look! God, you intoxicate me! I want to feel like a boy again. Come lie on top of me and fuck the wrinkles off my face. *(Silence.)* Dammit, Perdita, have a heart — I've worked my fingers to the bone! When I was a snot-nosed schoolboy I lived on bread and cold potatoes. Wore the same socks three weeks' running. Now I'm a respected M.P., a celebrated author, I dine with the Prince of Wales —

PERDITA. *(The newspaper.)* It says here the Committee on Public Ethics has found Lord Ryfact guilty of sleeping with his mother.

SHERIDAN. Are you listening to me?

PERDITA. It says she was eighty-three.

SHERIDAN. Charity begins at home.

PERDITA. They've sentenced him to be hanged. This is outrageous. Someone should speak out.

SHERIDAN. Against the Committee on Public Ethics? Against Mister Pitt?

PERDITA. What gives them the right to pass judgment like that?

SHERIDAN. It's our government, pet. That's what gives them the right.

PERDITA. And listen to this —

SHERIDAN. Don't be reading the paper while I'm trying to seduce you.

PERDITA. — There's to be a vote in the Commons in three weeks' time concerning the political situation in France.

SHERIDAN. Your eyes were meant for weeping, not for reading.

PERDITA. "The time has come for England to decide her allegiance — "

SHERIDAN. — Put it away.

PERDITA. " — She must either heed the call of the French King Louis — "

SHERIDAN. — I do not want to hear this!

PERDITA. " — Or come to the aid of the Jacobins in their cause for revolution."

SHERIDAN. *(Grabbing the newspaper away.)* That's enough!

PERDITA. There's your chance! Prove you're a man of substance. Prove you deserve my respect — take a stand in support of these rebels. *(Sheridan laughs.)* How can you laugh when people are dying? They're giving their lives to be free, Richard. Today it's France, tomorrow it could be here.

SHERIDAN. But Perdie — the French?

PERDITA. They're human beings!

SHERIDAN. Since when?

PERDITA. Richard, be a man.

SHERIDAN. Don't fret your pretty head about it. Right and just will always seize the day.

PERDITA. My mother died in filth and poverty while some rich nob took midnight supper off plates of gold. Tell me that was right and just. I've stood up on that stage and played empresses and queens — beneath their crowns and jewels, they are no better folk than me.

SHERIDAN. That's all very well, but there are larger issues to consider —

PERDITA. You supported the rebels in America during their campaign!

SHERIDAN. That was different.

PERDITA. Why? Because your wife was still alive? It's not enough you gave up writing, but you have to give up caring too? Let the world go to the shit-house as long as you keep what is yours!

SHERIDAN. One doesn't vote in Parliament to satisfy a nagging whore! *(Perdita slaps him.)* I'm sorry. Forgive me. Look, I'll consider it. I promise you. Now let's leave politics and think instead of congress. *(Sheridan begins kissing her neck and removing his jacket. Perdita spots a letter hanging in one of his pockets. She pulls it out.)*

PERDITA. What's this? Who's this from?

SHERIDAN. Give that back.

PERDITA. Scented paper, no less. Who is she?

SHERIDAN. None of your business.

PERDITA. What a beautiful seal. It'd be a pity to break it. Shall I break it? I think I should break it.

SHERIDAN. I'll break your neck — that is confidential business! *(Sheridan lunges at her. She spins. Picks up a knife and holds it out. Then brings it to the letter and is about to open it when she is distracted by —)*

HOPKINS. *(Off.)* Act one beginners, places please — curtain going up! *(In a split second, Sheridan grabs the letter back and puts it away.)*

PERDITA. You ape! I'd cut your heart out if you had one! I demand to — no, keep away! The play's about to start!

SHERIDAN. *(Lifting her skirts.)* You don't go on until scene two, so shut your face.

PERDITA. Richard, please — not here! Somebody might come!

SHERIDAN. That's what I'm hoping! *(And Sheridan disappears beneath her skirts. Perdita moans. The knife drops from her hands.*

Byron enters and remains by the door, unseen.)
PERDITA. *(Weakly.)* Oh, Richard, don't — stop — oh, Dick ... Dick! Dick! Dick! *(Byron clears his throat. Perdita squeals and runs off.)*
BYRON. I believe I have the honor of addressing Mister Sheridan?
SHERIDAN. You've got some bloody nerve.
BYRON. I have an appointment.
SHERIDAN. I suggest you keep it.
BYRON. Sir, it is important that we speak. I've come to warn you of a very delicate situation.
SHERIDAN. Christ and all his devils — Hopkins! You're not a writer, are you?
BYRON. Yes. Actually, sir, I am.
SHERIDAN. You got a handkerchief? *(Sheridan pulls a handkerchief from Byron's jacket and wipes his lips. Hopkins enters running. Music can be heard from offstage. It plays the duration of the scene.)*
HOPKINS. The curtain's up, sir. They can hear you on the stage.
SHERIDAN. I don't care if they hear me in the gods! Why isn't anyone minding the stage door? Show this man out! *(Hopkins holds out Perdita's undergarment. Sheridan grabs it and pockets it.)*
BYRON. There must be some mistake —
SHERIDAN. And shall I tell you what it is? If a writer can make his way backstage, then so can my creditors. Frankly, sir, I don't know which would be worse company.
BYRON. Sir, this is of the utmost urgency.
HOPKINS. Please step this way.
BYRON. You obviously don't recall our previous meeting.
SHERIDAN. I've never seen you before in my life.
BYRON. We met last week at the salon of Madame de Staël. I read you a poem of mine.
SHERIDAN. A naked lie! I never go near poetry. Doctor's orders.
HOPKINS. Shall I summon a constable, sir?
BYRON. *Childe Harold's Pilgrimage.* You said it showed great promise.
SHERIDAN. I must have been drunk. Is there a woman involved in this story?
HOPKINS. I'll fetch the constable.
BYRON. Never mind. I'll go.

SHERIDAN. No, wait! — That limp — of course! I remember now. The silly hair, the funny walk. Percy, isn't it?

BYRON. George.

SHERIDAN. Yes, that's it. George Percy.

BYRON. George Gordon, Lord Byron. I believe you're thinking of Shelley.

SHERIDAN. I knew there was a woman involved in this story!

PERDITA. *(Entering in full costume.)* It's Miss Pope — she heard you were in and said as soon as she's off she'll be coming directly to see you.

SHERIDAN. That vampire will suck me dry of every penny coming to her.

PERDITA. You stand up to her or pay her. One way or another, but I'm not lying for you again.

MISS POPE. *(Off.)* "Lydia! Come down here! Lydia, come down, I say!"

PERDITA. Christ, that's my cue — where's my fan?

SHERIDAN. Hopkins, do something!

HOPKINS. I'm only the stage manager, sir. No actress ever listens to me.

PERDITA. Where's my sodding fan?

SHERIDAN. *(To Byron.)* If an irate cow in a red wig comes looking for me, you must tell her I've gone.

BYRON. I cannot lie on your behalf, sir.

SHERIDAN. 'Course you can! You're a writer — it's your professional duty to lie!

MISS POPE. *(Off.)* "The little hussy won't hear — well, I'll go and tell her at once who it is."

SHERIDAN. Quick, hand me that tablecloth. The tablecloth! Now! *(To Byron.)* And you — get up on my shoulders.

BYRON. What?

SHERIDAN. I saw it in a play of Wycherly's. The play was a failure, but the device was a success. Climb on! *(As Byron straddles Sheridan's shoulders, Hopkins keeps watch at the door. Sheridan wraps Byron with the tablecloth so that Sheridan is concealed and it appears Byron is a very tall man.)*

MISS POPE. *(Off.)* "I don't wonder at your laughing. Ha! Ha! Ha!"

SHERIDAN. — And hand me that sausage!

17

MISS POPE. *(Off.)* " — Lydia, I say!" *(Perdita hands Sheridan a large sausage from the table. Hopkins hisses that Miss Pope is coming. Perdita gives Byron something to put atop his head and kisses Sheridan before Miss Pope enters in full costume.)* Where is that scurvy bitch? Get your ass on stage before I slit your — *(In shock at seeing the "giant.")* Mary mother of God.

PERDITA. Miss Pope, may I have the honor of introducing — uh —

HOPKINS. Uh — His Royal Highness ... the uh — Sultan of Rangoon.

BYRON. *(A bad accent.)* Ah, Miss Pope — I have traveled far and wide to feast my eyes on your great beauty. I wish to take you from this place and crown you queen of all my harems — *(Sheridan extends the sausage as the "giant" approaches. Miss Pope gasps and swoons and is dragged offstage gibbering as the "giant" exits.)*

Scene 3

A drinking room in Brooks, a private club. An ornate settee, candles. A loud ruckus as Charles James Fox, a fat and elderly man with a walking stick, enters followed by Sheridan and Byron. They are all drunk. Fox and Sheridan sing and Byron struggles to keep up.

SHERIDAN, FOX and BYRON. *(Singing.)*
"Let us take the road.
Hark! I hear the sound of coaches!
The hour of attack approaches,
T'your arms, brave boys, and load.
See the ball I hold!
Let the chymists toil like asses,
Our fire their fire surpasses
And turns all our lead to gold."

FOX. *(Toasting.)* Gentlemen, I give you — the prime minister!

18

SHERIDAN. *(Belches.)* The prime minister!

FOX. *(Belches.)* To a gentleman who occupies a very dear place in our heart —

SHERIDAN. — Like a tumor.

FOX. We dedicate this drink to the odious Mister Pitt —

SHERIDAN. — Alias Snake Pitt —

FOX. — Alias Pitiless Pitt —

SHERIDAN. — Alias Pitt without End —

BYRON. Get on with it!

SHERIDAN. To our loathsome and carbuncled Prime Minister —

FOX. — May his ethics committee be the death of him yet!

SHERIDAN. One — two — three — go! *(The three men chug their drinks in a race. Sheridan wins.)* Yes! Yes! Not as fast as you used to be, eh, Charlie? How many does this make? Six?

FOX. *(Coming in second.)* I thought seven. Or is it nine?

BYRON. *(Coming in third; winded:)* How do you gentlemen do it?

SHERIDAN. Charlie and I have shared the Whig Party bench for — what is it now? — Eighteen years?

FOX. Twenty.

SHERIDAN. — And although we have differed in opinion from time to time —

FOX. — Lord preserve us.

SHERIDAN. — There are two things on God's putrid earth we both proclaim as abhorrent. One is the malodorous Mister William Pitt, our execrable prime minister, and the other is —

FOX. *(Belching.)* Temperance!

SHERIDAN. Between Charlie and me, we could drink the Royal Navy under the table. What's the matter, George? You're looking a little wan.

FOX. Actually, he looks a big wan. Methinks your friend is not so well-equipped for the traditional Whig Party roister.

SHERIDAN. Alas, he is but green and lacks the seasoned spleen that age —

FOX. — And girth —

SHERIDAN and FOX. — Provide. *(Sheridan and Fox belch in each other's faces. It is an old game.)*

BYRON. You still haven't answered my question, Mister Sheridan.

FOX. *(Sitting.)* 'Sdeath, sir, let it go!

BYRON. I do not understand how you can be so complacent!

SHERIDAN. What's not to understand? Look — plays are made by writers; writing implies structure; structure implies tradition; tradition implies morality. I have no morality; ipso facto, I am no writer.

BYRON. But you were! You can't escape your past.

SHERIDAN. I can try to escape my future.

BYRON. To deprive the world of pleasure? To rob your promise its fulfillment — ?

SHERIDAN. All right, then ask me again.

BYRON. Why did you give up writing?

SHERIDAN. None of your fucking business! There. I'm a rude old bastard so you can piss off or buy the next round.

FOX. Here, here!

BYRON. Where has your passion gone? Your genius was unrivaled — each word you penned, like silver constellations, lit and brightened the night sky. How could you turn your back? Surely you can remember what it was that made you write. I do it because I want to change the world. Yes, go on and laugh. But my aspirations are deeper than surface values such as personal gain.

SHERIDAN. Charlie, do we want to change the world?

FOX. No, we don't.

SHERIDAN. Do we like surface values?

FOX. Yes, we do.

SHERIDAN. This is why we're in politics.

BYRON. But the whole point of politics is to make a difference. To create a world worth living in. To cause action. As a man of the theatre I thought you would know. In the theatre, action is everything.

SHERIDAN. The theatre, my boy, is just a little room where people come to hear the latest gossip. As for politics — it's even more divine. Speaking for hours and never saying a thing, making promises which never need be kept —

FOX. — Skimming the cream and pissing in the milk.

SHERIDAN. That's the life of an M.P. — Misleading Pretense.

BYRON. Moral Prostitution.

FOX. Monstrous Prick. *(He belches loudly.)*

BYRON. You're not the man I thought you were.

SHERIDAN. What man ever is? My boy, writing is for people who don't want to live their own lives.

BYRON. Not so — it is for people in search of truth.

SHERIDAN. Thus spake a poet. The truth, my lad, is nothing but a whore.

BYRON. Is there nothing you hold of value? Is there nothing you believe in?

SHERIDAN. Retribution. Death. And women with large breasts.

FOX. Where? *(Looks around; disappointed:)* Oh. *(He belches.)*

BYRON. Mister Sheridan, you're a fraud.

SHERIDAN. Oh, how all you eager aspiring writers love to spout ideals — how this is wrong and that is wrong and this is how it should be. But tell me, lad, what happens when you reach your summit — when you get what you wish for? All these hopes and ideals — what then? What happens when you wake one day and it's all there in your hand — be it a successful play, or a seat in government, or even love? What happens when you see the awfulness of the fact that reality can never live up to your dreams — that every striving leads to disappointment — that the world is a lump of shite. You see, I once believed as you do. Oh yes, I was full of the hope and anger of youth. Looking at you reminds me too much of what I once had. Looking at me, you're seeing your future. So look carefully, George, and tell me — what's the fucking point?

BYRON. That was the most repulsive sentiment I've ever heard man utter.

FOX. There's only one thing I want to know. Who's buying the next round?

SHERIDAN. You're the only one who understands me, Charlie. Him and Perdita, they'll drive me off the drink.

FOX. Sherry — woman trouble?

SHERIDAN. First it's a new play she's after. Now she wants me to campaign for the Jacobins.

FOX. Oh, now, when a tottie sticks her muzzle into politics, that's when she earns a good kick in the teeth.

SHERIDAN. Oh, but you don't know this woman. I catch myself in her eyes and I feel young again — what's the word on the benches, Charlie? If the party is backing the rebels, I'll vote with the fold and everything works out for the best.

BYRON. That's right. Follow the fleet and never think for yourself.

SHERIDAN. Every hand washes another.

BYRON. Every ass gets kissed. Whose bunghole do you worship, Mister Fox?

FOX. *(Staring at Byron, coldly:)* Look here — who *are* you?

SHERIDAN. He's an annoying little turd who's applying for the job of being my conscience.

BYRON. I only do it because the position has been vacant for so long.

FOX. What do you think politics is? Altruism? Look, mate, it's bloody fucking work and we're not in this for a sainthood. As for this vote, Sherry, I'd be careful if I were you. There's a Tory rumor going round. Something about setting the prince up with a Catholic or something. Doesn't sound good.

SHERIDAN. Where'd you hear this?

FOX. I know Prinnie's done you a few favors — put money in your theatre and that — but if any of this came to light, Mister Pitt wouldn't look too kindly on it. I'd be careful where I tread. Enough rumors can topple a man.

SHERIDAN. Are you telling me not to support the Jacobins, Charlie?

FOX. I'm telling you to lay quiet for a while. People remember the old days. They haven't forgotten your voice — how you used to orate and speechify. Silver-tongued Sheridan, they called you. You come out in favor of the rebels — you get Pitt angry over this vote and he'll stop at nothing. He'll root out every rumor and that committee of his will be on your back like vultures on a dead man.

SHERIDAN. I can't believe I'm hearing this. What about the party? They'll be expecting my support.

FOX. I'm speaking as your friend.

SHERIDAN. After twenty years you'd have me back the royals? This isn't you at all.

BYRON. I say vote your conscience and do right by the people. Damn the gossipmongers and their hateful rumors.

FOX. Who asked your opinion?

BYRON. Revolution's in the air, Mister Fox. Look at America!

FOX. Ha! America's a nonsense!

BYRON. All men are created and born equal.

FOX. That's as may be. But they don't live equal and they never will.

BYRON. One must strive, for without striving, there is no progress and no hope. The world is full of beauty. It's up to us to set it free.

FOX. I wouldn't trust him, Sherry. He talks like a rebel himself — and look at the way he walks!

SHERIDAN. He's got a clubfoot, for Christ sake!

FOX. *(Suspicious.)* Ah! And how'd he get it?

BYRON. Mister Fox, it is a birth defect.

SHERIDAN. Charlie understands. Charlie *is* a birth defect.

FOX. You think it's all a joke, do you? I witnessed a hanging today. Lord Ryfact. You should have been there to see it, Sherry. That was the work of Pitt's committee. That was the work of a rumor. The Duchess of Devonshire ruined that man.

BYRON. The Duchess of Devonshire?

FOX. If you won't do it for yourself, Richard, then do it for me.

SHERIDAN. You? What has this to do with — George, you look pale. Are you ill?

FOX. What you say — what you do — your actions have consequences.

SHERIDAN. This is nonsense. I'm toeing the party line! — George?

FOX. Just because some flaming actress tells you how to vote —

BYRON. I think I'm going to be sick.

FOX. — Some piss-pot tupenny whore —

SHERIDAN. *(Trying to laugh it off.)* All right, Charlie, I think you've had your fun.

FOX. Loyalty, integrity, that's what makes a man. You haven't got a spine!

SHERIDAN. I haven't time for this. I've got some business to —

FOX. *(To Byron.)* You look up to him? You idolize this man? Let me tell you about your Richard Sheridan. His definition of loyalty includes stepping on a friend, includes killing his own wife!

SHERIDAN. By Christ, Charlie, you will cross the line!

FOX. He had her slaving in that theatre — doing accounts and running errands. Consumption he says — bollocks! He worked her to death.

SHERIDAN. I warn you!

FOX. That woman was an angel. Oh, to hear her sing — the voice she had — !

SHERIDAN. Enough!

FOX. Use your friends and toss 'em in a dung heap, that's your fucking motto! *(Sheridan strikes Fox in the face. He falls. Byron steps in to restrain Sheridan.)*

BYRON. Gentlemen — Richard — no. This is no way to —

SHERIDAN. He don't know when to shut his hole. *(Pause.)* I'm all right. Come on, Charlie, let me help you up. Give me your hand. *(Fox spits into Sheridan's hand.)* Ah. Now she's pouting. *(Pause.)* Well I'll be buggered if I care. I'm off. I've got a letter to deliver.

BYRON. Richard, you mustn't leave like this —

FOX. It's that business with the prince — I was right!

SHERIDAN. For Christ sake, what's come over you?

FOX. If Pitt ever found out —

SHERIDAN. Never tell me what's good for me, Charlie. I won't listen!

BYRON. *(Stopping Sheridan.)* Wait — don't go. You should stay and see this through. Mister Fox is your friend.

FOX. That man is no friend of mine.

BYRON. Gentlemen, come — after twenty years? Look at yourselves. This isn't right. Give me the letter. I'll deliver it for you.

SHERIDAN. I couldn't do that, George.

BYRON. Is an errand worth the price of friendship?

FOX. He's after something. I can feel it in my bones.

BYRON. Mister Fox, it is the guilty man who has suspicion on his mind.

FOX. And what do you mean by that? I'll box your fucking ears, boy!

BYRON. Gentlemen, forgive me. I meant to help but I have overstepped my bounds.

FOX. Him and that actress, filling your head with ideas — revolution, rebellion, upheaval — who are you going to listen to, Richard — a perfect stranger you don't know from Adam or me that knows you inside and out?

SHERIDAN. *(Pause. Thinks. Hands Byron the letter.)* Thirty-four, The Strand. Deliver it in person. Go now.

BYRON. Yes, sir. Right away. *(Exits.)*

FOX. You'll let spite make you a fool? You'd better pray that you can trust him, Richard. It doesn't take much to turn a man into a Judas.

SHERIDAN. Truly, Charlie — are you speaking from experience? *(A commotion offstage. Cries of "The King of France arrested! Long live the revolution!" and the sound of shattering glass. Fox and Sheridan stare at each other as the lights fade and the cries grow louder. Byron appears and hands the letter to the Duchess of Devonshire. They vanish as a scream fills the darkness —)*

Scene 4

The cry is that of William Pitt, waking from a nightmare in his sweat-soaked nightclothes. He is a pale, thin-lipped, and unhealthy-looking man. He breathes. He calms. As he speaks, Servants enter and proceed to dress, wig, and powder him.

PITT. You step into the sun and at first the glare is enough to blind you — committees, depositions, legislation, policies foreign and domestic, constituencies demanding to be heard. All around, the savage buzz of history unfolding in your blood. It is overwhelming — like a fever. Avoiding history is avoiding one's own breath. In my nightmares, the world is cold steel awash in a sea of red. I fight. I fight. Ours is a country of infinite symbols — Stonehenge — the Magna Carta — the Chair of Kings sat in by William the Conqueror. These are the bindings of our national spirit. They must be upheld. My administration, like history, is built on strength. On the symbols that have shaped and conquered. Strength is a simple beast. It lives on a diet of other people's fear. History is infinite but fickle. My government is definite and driven. History doesn't give a damn what choice you make so long as you make it. *(Fully dressed and powdered, Pitt turns upstage and steps into the antechamber to the King's bedroom in the palace. George III sits in a wheelchair, asleep. Covering his face is a damp cloth. Mrs. Crewe leaves his side and approaches Pitt.)*

MRS. CREWE. He should sleep a while now, Mister Pitt.

PITT. And the queen?

MRS. CREWE. She's stolen the sugar canister from the kitchen and locked herself in her closet with the footman.

PITT. You'd better tend to her, Mrs. Crewe. And see the footman is roundly whipped. We don't want him talking. It's like a nursery around here today. *(Mrs. Crewe exits. Pitt sighs, pulls a handkerchief from the King's pocket, and mops his own brow. Fox enters. He is dressed formally and carries a silver-tipped walking stick, instead of his old wooden one. He bows to the king.)* The king sleeps, Mister Fox. You may approach.

FOX. The newspapers reported his condition had improved.

PITT. Far too many people view his illness as a weakness of the system.

FOX. And so you fabricate reports?

PITT. It is not fabrication, Mister Fox. It is utilizing facts to their best advantage. See how peacefully he rests?

GEORGE III. *(Waking, groaning, blowing on the cloth, causing it to flutter.)* What? Who's there? What what — *(Pitt uncovers the king's face.)* Ah. Veronica — what —

PITT. He has been laboring under the delusion that Saint Veronica attends him.

FOX. Saint Veronica?

PITT. The maid that mopped our Savior's brow on his journey to the cross.

GEORGE III. Damn this mumbling — what —

PITT. Mister Fox, your majesty. *(Fox bows. The king eyes him suspiciously.)*

GEORGE III. A pox on him, what does he want?

PITT. It is we who want, your majesty.

GEORGE III. *Ach — ja, ja, natürlich.* What do we want?

PITT. The vote, your majesty. The vote in Parliament.

GEORGE III. Kill it!

FOX. Your majesty?

26

GEORGE III. Kill the bloody beast! What's a goat doing in Parliament? It's enough with frogs about everywhere! *(Spits on the floor.)*

PITT. *(To Fox.)* The French.

GEORGE III. *Ach, sehr schlecht!* They're a nasty bunch, Veronica. Smelly. Especially what's-his-name — the ugly one —

PITT. Robespierre, your majesty.

GEORGE III. *(Spits on the floor.)* So he's gone and bought himself a goat, what —

PITT. Not a goat, Your Majesty. The *vote.*

GEORGE III. Ah.

PITT. Charles Fox is your representative from the borough of Westminster. Though not a Tory, he has been lobbying the Commons to ensure us unanimous support of the French monarchy during the upcoming foreign-policy vote.

GEORGE III. Ah.

PITT. The Jacobin rebels have overtaken the National Assembly and imprisoned the King of France. This coup must be stopped. On no account must Britain recognize this band of brigands with their so-called "Rights of Man."

GEORGE III. Ah. Why?

PITT. It would lead decent Englishmen to question our own system and undermine the people's trust in the Crown.

GEORGE III. Do you trust the Crown, Veronica?

PITT. I do, Your Majesty.

GEORGE III. You should try wearing it sometime — it's bloody heavy. Julius Caesar, now he was a lucky bastard. Got to wear a shrubbery on his head. Tell me, when do I get to see the goat? *(Pitt covers the king's face with the cloth.)* Veronica! What's happened? It's dark!

FOX. They say he's been like this ever since he lost the thirteen colonies out in —

PITT. *(Raising a hand in warning; stopping him.)* You must never mention the name of that place in front of His Majesty. It has an ill effect.

GEORGE III. I'm scared of the dark!

PITT. So tell me, Fox, have you secured for us Mister Sheridan?

FOX. I need more time.

PITT. That is not what I want to hear. You assured me that there would be no problem here.

FOX. There is no problem, sir. Only it's difficult to — well, to pin him down. One moment it's Whig solidarity and the next ... He likes to ruffle feathers.

PITT. Our country is not a goose. I don't enjoy your analogy. I have taken soundings and know the intentions of every other member of the House in regard to this vote. The scales are evenly weighted. We are running neck and neck. The only one left to hear from is your friend Mister Sheridan and I don't like a loose cannon. Especially one as gifted at swaying public opinion as he is. What have you heard about these rumors circulating?

FOX. Rumors, Prime Minister?

PITT. About Sheridan and the prince. Find out what you can. They may prove useful in pressuring him into place. I want him on my side. I will not lose this battle.

FOX. He's a sworn member of the opposition.

PITT. So were you, Mister Fox.

FOX. Yes, and I can't help feeling —

PITT. Like a traitor? Spare me your petty theatricals. You are not being paid to feel. You are paid to act. Perhaps I was wrong to approach you. Perhaps you're not the man we need in Westminster after the next election.

FOX. Is that a threat? I won't be bullied, sir. It's true I need your help, but don't presume to threaten me. I am a man of power.

PITT. No — you were. Your muscle's gone. You want to rise again? Then you'd do well to listen. There's a structure here at stake. A way of living which has done well by us all. *(The king begins to moan and whimper. Pitt snatches the cloth from his face, frightening him. The king sucks his thumb.)* Look on your monarch, sir. His ancestors ruled long before your birth and his descendants will rule long after your death. At this moment in history, he suffers. He needs you. We need you. Sometimes a country's optimum path leads across a few people's toes. This can't be helped. But the end always justifies the means. That is patriotism. It is that simple. Now I need Sheridan's vote. Is that clear?

FOX. Yes, sir. And the election? Mister Wilberforce is poised to overtake me. I need your endorsement, Prime Minister. You will help me keep my seat?

PITT. If you are worthy of my endorsement then you shall have it. But you must earn that worth.

GEORGE III. Look, Veronica — it's sunset time!

MRS. CREWE. *(Entering.)* I've put her to bed, Prime Minister.

PITT. Any trouble?

MRS. CREWE. She screamed a bit and scratched a chambermaid's face, but I gave her a tea cake and that's kept her quiet.

PITT. Good. And the footman?

MRS. CREWE. A fractured hip and a broken jaw. He won't talk.

GEORGE III. Take me to the sunset, Veronica. I want to see it happen.

MRS. CREWE. *(Indicating the king.)* Shall I — ?

PITT. I'll do it myself, Mrs. Crewe. I expect results, Mister Fox. Don't let me see you again until you've done what I've asked.

FOX. You have my word on it, sir. *(Pitt hands Fox a pouch of money and wheels the king off, with Mrs. Crewe following. Fox juggles the pouch of coins in his hand.)* — My word. *(Fox exits.)*

Scene 5

A clearing in St. James' Park. Moonlight. The sound of distant horseshoes on pavement. Byron can be heard approaching. As he recites, he enters with Perdita. Both are dancing and giddy. Sheridan follows.

BYRON.
  "Our love is fixed, I think we've proved it,
    Nor time, nor place, nor art have moved it;
    Then wherefore should we sigh and whine,
    With groundless jealousy repine,
    With silly whims and fancies frantic — "
SHERIDAN. *(To Perdita.)* Why not?
PERDITA. Shush! Behave yourself!

BYRON.
 "Merely to make our love romantic?
 Why should you weep like Lydia Languish,
 And fret with self-created anguish?"
PERDITA. Oh, Dick — Lydia Languish — from your play *The Rivals.*
BYRON.
 "Or doom the lover you have chosen,
 On winter nights to sigh half frozen,"
SHERIDAN. *Now* will you tell me why?
BYRON. Am I boring you, sir?
PERDITA. Pay no attention to Mister Snotty. Please — go on.
BYRON. "Or doom the lover you have chosen — "
SHERIDAN. You did that bit.
BYRON.
 "On winter nights to sigh half frozen;
 In leafless shades to sue for pardon,
 Only because the scene's a garden?"
(Perdita applauds. Byron bows in mock ceremony.)
PERDITA. That was wonderful! Oh, wasn't it wonderful, Richard?
BYRON. It's supposed to be a — well, an homage of sorts. To the great lost talent of Richard Sheridan.
SHERIDAN. Oh, you're good.
BYRON. My intention was to inspire something in you.
SHERIDAN. Nausea and exhaustion.
PERDITA. What about all those people gathered round listening to his every word? Didn't it fill you with a desire to rush home and grab up your pen?
SHERIDAN. The only thing I hate more than poetry is a literary salon. Don't misunderstand me, George, I'm very happy about your book being published. But seven times tonight — seven times — I was asked "So, Sherry, when are you going to give us another play?" And all of them clicking their tongues and looking down their beaks at me as if I were some forgotten relic.
BYRON. You play the part so well that no one can tell the difference anymore.
PERDITA. He's right. When *are* you going to quit playing dog in

the manger and give us another play? Talk to him, George. You're a good influence.

SHERIDAN. Talk to *her*, George. She'll listen to you.

PERDITA. And what should he say that you can't?

SHERIDAN. It's not what I can't say but what you won't hear! Do you know what I did tonight, George, between the poetry and the *pâté?* I proposed to this woman! That's right — marriage! And she giggled in my face! If you weren't so beautiful, my dear, I'd break your fucking neck. Do you want me on bended knee like a boy of seventeen? I will! *(Goes down on bended knee.)*

PERDITA. Oh, stop it, you selfish little man! Marry you indeed — what of my life? My wishes? My career?

SHERIDAN. I'm offering you my heart and soul — !

BYRON. A bloated liver and a lump of coal!

PERDITA. Suppose I said yes — suppose I married you — what then? What would my future hold? Staying home all day, tucked neatly between the sheets, awaiting your manly arrival?

SHERIDAN. Most women would consider that an honor.

PERDITA. Or slaving over your account books till I drop just like your wife. *(Silence.)*

BYRON. Another poem anyone?

SHERIDAN. Perdita, I need you.

PERDITA. — Yes, as a flower needs the sun; as a child needs his mother; as a drunkard needs his drink. You need me as long as I give of myself, but what do I get? Love is not without condition, Richard.

SHERIDAN. Never get involved with an actress, George. She may look you lovingly in the eye, but all she sees is her own reflection.

PERDITA. You're an absurd man, Dick Sheridan. Now it's late and I'm cold and I want to go home. Good night, George. Congratulations on your book. *(Perdita shakes Byron's hand. She turns to Sheridan and kisses his forehead.)* I'll see you at the theatre, little man. *(Perdita exits. Sheridan slumps. Byron watches her go.)*

BYRON. There goes a shockingly fine woman.

SHERIDAN. She's a cunt. I'm in love with a stupid cunt!

BYRON. I wouldn't call that love, Richard.

SHERIDAN. Oh? And what would you, Master Poet of the Hour?

BYRON. Desperation and ingratitude.

SHERIDAN. Get stuffed.

BYRON. Do you dismiss everyone who sees the best in you?

SHERIDAN. All right, George — enough! You can quit pretending now. What — you think I'm blind? You think I haven't sussed you out? Oh yes, I'm on to you. Tell me your secret.

BYRON. Secret? What —

SHERIDAN. I've watched you, boy. I know.

BYRON. *(Pause.)* Oh God, how did you — ?

SHERIDAN. That's right. She's a married woman, isn't she?

BYRON. *(Pause.)* What?

SHERIDAN. Lady Caroline Lamb. *(Pause. Byron begins to laugh with nervous relief. He can't stop.)* All night long — she couldn't keep her hands off you. Women swarmed about you like a gaggle of randy chickens while I stood by like a pillar of salt. How do you do it? What is so blastedly funny? Stop it!

BYRON. *(Laughing.)* I'm sorry. I thought you — never mind. I'm sorry.

SHERIDAN. They want you — your mind, your body —

BYRON. Women can't resist a man who ignores them completely.

SHERIDAN. You don't realize what a lucky man you are.

BYRON. They want what they *think* I am.

SHERIDAN. Appearances are everything.

BYRON. It's all a lie. *(Pause.)* And you — squandering your gifts as though they grow on trees. She was right — You are ridiculous to debase yourself upon the ground. If you spent *half* the time you do chasing skirt and wine on that which makes you great, you'd *own* this world! You were everything I saw as bright and noble in man's heart, but — oh, why do I even bother trying? A fine pair of liars we are.

SHERIDAN. Wait! — I know a shortcut through the park — we'll catch her up. You'll help me change her mind.

BYRON. For Christ sake, Richard, let Perdita be!

SHERIDAN. I need your help, my friend. You're the only one who understands me. Come! It's not too late! Quickly! Quickly! *(Sheridan exits running. Byron follows after a beat. Prinnie enters, followed by the Duchess of Devonshire. They both wear stylized half-masks which conceal the upper halves of their faces. Prinnie is a young man, foppishly dressed. The Duchess of Devonshire is in black.)*

PRINNIE. Pish, madam, let me be! I've told you I can't love you. If I ever said I did, it was a cruel and heartless joke.

DEVONSHIRE. You quote yourself quite well.

PRINNIE. I meant every word of that letter — every letter of each word. It is over between us!

DEVONSHIRE. If it were love I was after, I certainly wouldn't come to you. But a promise is a promise, and marriage not a thing to be taken lightly, especially for one in your position.

PRINNIE. Pish!

DEVONSHIRE. You pledged to me your hand.

PRINNIE. There — sever it and take it. The rest you shall not have!

DEVONSHIRE. Hell's bells, Prinnie — be sensible! A Catholic widow? 'Sdeath! How can you risk your future for a mangy piece of papist tat? I know you better than you know yourself. You've no intention of completing this charade!

PRINNIE. I suppose my alternative is with you? And end up like my father? He married a fortune hunter. Yesterday he locked himself in the airing cupboard screaming about mice — he thinks he's a piece of Swiss cheese. Pah! The only reason you hold to this claim is that you've reached that age unmarried women of the court so dread. Without your looks or any husband, you'll have no power left at all. Bereft, you'll wash up on shore by the uncaring tide, an unloved and decaying slab — while I have found true bliss that neither wind nor weather can corrupt.

DEVONSHIRE. I once thought love made men fools. Now I see they are born that way. For God's sake, Prinnie — love who you may, I am a better match than she!

PRINNIE. Pish and pish again! Why can't you see that every aspect of your person so repulses me — your face, your shape, your voice ... I am to meet Maria here at any moment, but that sticky-sweet perfume of yours has made me feel so sick that I've completely lost my bearings and do not know where I am. I will leave you now. I suggest that you desist from thus pursuing me. *(Prinnie exits.)*

DEVONSHIRE. I am a persistent woman — I will have what's rightly mine! How dare you walk away from me? Prinnie? Prinnie! *(Devonshire exits, pursuing. Sheridan storms on with Byron following.)*

SHERIDAN. If you say "I told you so," I'll rip your bollocks off and shove them down your throat.

BYRON. For God's sake, Richard. It's not my fault she slammed the window in your face. *(Pause.)* Even though I told you so — *(Sheridan growls and chases a laughing Byron around the stage. Finally winded, he stops.)*

SHERIDAN. I need a drink. I'd like to crawl into a hole and pull it right in after me.

BYRON. I know what sort of hole you'd like to crawl into. You'll kill yourself if you go on like this.

SHERIDAN. Hope springs eternal. *(Sees Byron giving him a look.)* What! You think I wanted to end up like this? I look back on my days and wish I could erase them all. I lie awake at night, wanting to reach a hand inside my skull to rip the memories from my brain.

BYRON. You mustn't dwell upon the sadness of the past. It serves no purpose, Richard.

SHERIDAN. Sadness? *(Laughing.)* It's happiness one must forget. Memories of pleasures past have more venom in their sting than any deep-inflicted wound. My youth was near delirious! A fairy book of charm and light and certainty. *(Silence.)* Have you ever experienced beauty, George? A beauty so intense and so unbearable it pains the heart to look upon? There are no words for it. No words that I could ever pen. I see her, you know. Eliza. Usually, it's just the train of a gown turning a corner. Or the tilt of a hat, just so, from behind. I'll think I've forgotten and be walking down a street and there she is in the folds and flutters of a lady's fan. My breath catches. I run up. I look. It's never her. And then I'll know once more that she is buried in the damp cold ground. She was my gem and I tossed her in the mud and there's no forgiveness in the world for that. Oh, what a mawkish parody of man I have become. I will confess, I've thought of putting pen to paper once again. I find myself wondering what it would be like to stand in Parliament and speak with deep conviction as I once did. But could my small and hollow words make any difference when I've lost what I believe? Now all that's left are the motions and gestures. What if there is nothing beyond them? What if there never was? What if it's all been emptiness behind a fancy show — a wicked play of words with no meaning and no heart?

BYRON. Stop it! Stop it — why are you telling me these things?

SHERIDAN. I thought you poets valued truth.

BYRON. How can I stand here, listening to this — this — if you but knew the truth, you would not call me "friend."

SHERIDAN. Have I said something to distress you?

BYRON. I thought you'd given up! I thought, what difference could it make? A man who sees no hope cannot be hurt. I'd watch you swilling, whoring and all the while I'd think, what harm is there? He doesn't care. But oh, you do! For where there's doubt, there's hope and — oh, good God, what have I done?

SHERIDAN. George, you're raving.

BYRON. I'd never seek to hurt you, Richard. I'd never look to harm. Not with intent. You do believe that, don't you?

SHERIDAN. Yes, of course.

BYRON. Then listen, please — this vote — don't go. You mustn't speak. Abstain. Be undecided. Drink — go on a bender — anything — but promise me you won't!

SHERIDAN. You've changed your tune.

BYRON. Don't you understand? If you should write again, if you speak out in Parliament, if there's one glimmer yet of faith in you, then I have trampled on the only truth that I believe in!

SHERIDAN. George, I do not understand.

BYRON. You've got to swear! Swear to me you won't!

SHERIDAN. All right! All right! I swear!

BYRON. I was so wrong about you, Richard. I've done a terrible thing.

SHERIDAN. You're still young. You can afford to be wrong about most everything. Now whatever this nasty business is, it's all behind you. Cheer up, lad. You must not so dolefully anticipate the past. Instead, let your retrospection be all to the future. *(Byron laughs in spite of himself.)* There now. You go home and get some rest. You'll feel better in the morning.

BYRON. Each word of kindness that you speak is like a burning cinder in my heart.

SHERIDAN. Are you going to start with the poetry again? I'll kick your bloody backside! Now go home! Go! Good night! *(Byron exits. Sheridan remains. Suddenly, a massive rumbling of voices off-stage and a gavel strikes sharply three times —)*

Scene 6

*Charles Fox can be heard over the din as beautifully deco-
rated walls appear out of the darkness —*

FOX. Mister Speaker, if I may be allowed to continue — *(The gavel
sounds again and the voices hush. A sliver of light illuminates Fox high
above.)* It is my duty as a member of this House — nay, as an
Englishman — to put aside all partisan concern and warn my right
honorable colleagues who are contemplating this debate that our
country is presently becoming a refuge to the fleeing hordes of the
French nobility seeking their asylum here from the bloodbath and
the carnage taking place in their homeland. Unless we take imme-
diate action to quash this mad rebellion overseas and help restore the
order of the monarchy, our shores will overrun with Frenchmen.
Can we provide for them? Have we the money or resources for these
refugees? More to the point, dear gentlemen — do we even *want*
them here? *(Wild cries of "No! No!" as lights fade on Fox and rise
downstage: a reception room off the main hall of the House of
Commons. Large portraits hang floor to ceiling. Prominent among these
are those of King George III and Queen Sophia-Charlotte. There are
large double doors up center and a terrace down right. A table with bottles of wine. George III is wheeled in by Mrs. Crewe. He wears his finest
military uniform, though a blanket covers his legs.)*
GEORGE III. Damn this noise — what —
MRS. CREWE. That is our government, Your Majesty. The
House of Commons. Just beyond those doors.
GEORGE III. Commons? Government? Rubbish! I am the king
— what — defender of the faith and master of the realm. If foreign
foe by sea or land should threat this mighty land of — land of —
DEVONSHIRE. *(Entering.)* England?
GEORGE III. *Ja, ja — natürlich!* Who are you?
MRS. CREWE. Your Majesty remembers the Duchess of
Devonshire.

DEVONSHIRE.   A word, Mrs. Crewe? *(Mrs. Crewe wheels the King upstage.)*

GEORGE III.   Where are you taking me?

MRS. CREWE.   Has Your Majesty seen your new portrait? It's most becoming.

GEORGE III.   Looks like a box of farts. Who is it? *(Mrs. Crewe rejoins the Duchess, leaving the King. They speak in hushed tones.)*

DEVONSHIRE.   They've set the date. The marriage is planned for a fortnight Thursday. I'm counting on you to keep him alive for at least another month.

MRS. CREWE.   Charlotte, I can't do this anymore. The doctors say his heart is weakening. The slightest shock might finish him.

DEVONSHIRE.   Then why did you bring him here? You must convince him to leave at once.

MRS. CREWE.   Believe me, I try. But he's impossible. He's got it in his head to remind Parliament of what they're fighting for.

DEVONSHIRE.   Rose, if Prinnie marries that woman my influence in court is gone. As long as His Majesty is alive, he still has influence on his son. Talk to him. I know he listens to you.

MRS. CREWE.   I mention your name at every opportunity, but he doesn't seem to understand. He thinks his son is a turnip! I can't take this pressure anymore. I wake up in the night sweating. I can't eat. I can't think. I tremble at the slightest noise. Please, Charlotte — leave all this. I beg you — for my life!

DEVONSHIRE.   *(Stroking Crewe's cheek.)* Soon. Soon, Rose. I promise.

GEORGE III.   *(Cowlike.)* Mmmmoooo!

MRS. CREWE.   Your Majesty?

GEORGE III.   Who's the cow with the great big udders?

MRS. CREWE.   That isn't a cow, your majesty. That is the queen, your wife. *(Loud cries of assent and approval offstage as the center doors open and Pitt enters, followed by Fox.)*

PITT.   A sterling speech, Mister Fox. We've got them by the throat!

FOX.   If I could have a moment of your time —

PITT.   *(Seeing the King.)* What the devil's going on? What's he doing here?

MRS. CREWE.   The king has come to address the House, Prime Minister.

GEORGE III. I have come to see the goat!

PITT. Now, now, Your Majesty, you really oughtn't be here. Why don't you let the lovely Mrs. Crewe return you to the palace.

GEORGE III. I want to speak! I've brought my lucky carrot! *(The king brandishes a large carrot.)*

PITT. No, no, Your Majesty. I can't allow you in there.

GEORGE III. Do you dare defy your king? I order you to stand aside! Drive on, my dear — Drive on! *(Pitt steps aside. Mrs. Crewe wheels the king off as he holds up his lucky carrot. The Duchess of Devonshire follows. Like a goat; exiting.)* Bbb-eee-hhh!

PITT. Dammit all to hell!

FOX. Mister Pitt, please — I need to ask you —

PITT. If he should open up his mouth in there, he'll turn my cause into a laughingstock. They'll take one look at Farmer George and ask themselves if a monarchy is worth defending after all.

FOX. You said my speech fulfilled its purpose, sir. I need to know that I can count on your endorsement for my reelection campaign.

PITT. Mister Fox, at this moment I am less concerned with your paltry little campaign than I am with that Prussian pig-sticker destroying the majority I've worked so hard to gain. If he loses me any more than five seats, the game is up. So you had better deliver me Sheridan or we're lost — and that includes your reelection.

FOX. I turned my back on a life's allegiance for you. I betrayed my party's call. Surely you can give me some assurance that you'll stand by me — at the very least as a friend.

PITT. A friend? This is business, Mister Fox. If it's a friend you're after, I suggest you try your local whorehouse. You get me this vote and I will see what I can do. In the meantime I suggest you campaign with your constituency. Kiss a few babies, fuck a few widows. Only don't press the matter with me. *(Pitt exits through the double doors. Laughter can be heard from within. Fox goes to the table and drinks. Sheridan enters quietly through one of the double doors. An awkward moment between the two men. Sheridan takes a bottle of wine and goes to the terrace. He looks out.)*

SHERIDAN. Would you care to join me in a drink, Charlie? *(Hesitantly, Fox goes to Sheridan's side. They stand looking out and up.)* Starry night. *(Pause. Fox looks away.)* You all right?

FOX. I can't look up. I get dizzy.

SHERIDAN. *(Handing Fox the bottle.)* Here. *(Fox drinks. Hands the bottle back. Sheridan drinks.)*

FOX. When I was a lad, I read in a book that court astrologers used to search the skies for a new star to name after their king. I used to fancy finding one. I'd keep it a secret to myself.

SHERIDAN. The North Fox. Something like that? *(Pause.)* And did you?

FOX. Once. It was a shooting star.

SHERIDAN. They're supposed to be lucky.

FOX. It fell. Shot across the sky, burned itself out, and fell. *(Pause.)* I betrayed you, Richard. You, the party, everything I ever worked for. He was very good to me at first. Almost like a courtship. He promised to endorse my reelection — *if* I could ensure that you would —

SHERIDAN. Vote against the rebels.

FOX. It's a way of life, isn't it — the royals. Who are we to judge a system that has lasted for hundreds of years? All my life I've fought against them and everything they stand for. When you fight something your whole life, you grow to depend on it for your own survival. And now I find I need them more than ever and I am ashamed. Can you understand?

SHERIDAN. Yes. Yes, I can.

FOX. Truly? I knew you would. I said to him, "Sherry will understand." I said, "You can count on him to know what side his bread is buttered." I *can* count on you, can't I? As a friend?

SHERIDAN. *(Pause. Looking at Fox.)* Good-bye, Charlie. *(Turns to go.)*

FOX. What — Richard — wait — you *will* do this for me, won't you? You wouldn't turn your back on me? Not after I've confessed!

SHERIDAN. You could have asked me, Charlie. After twenty years, you could have simply asked. You didn't just betray me or the party — you betrayed yourself.

FOX. Fucking hell, Richard — you want me to beg? I'll beg. There — on my knees. Don't leave me like this! I had to do something. My position has become unstable. The voters no longer respect me.

SHERIDAN. Can you honestly blame them? Look at yourself, Charlie. You're a disgrace. *(Sheridan exits. Fox yells after him.)*

FOX. I'll tell him everything! I'll drag you down! Richard

Sheridan, royal pimp! *(He weeps.)*

PRINNIE. *(Off; overlapping:)* Father! Where is that wrinkled scalawag? Father! *(Fox cries, rocking in place. Prinnie storms on, drunk and furious.)* I know you're here — I'll shake you out of this monkey-house yet! Teach you to meddle in my affairs — *(Prinnie exits opposite, crashing into Byron as he enters.)* Out of my way! Father!

BYRON. Mister Fox? *(Rushing to his side.)* Mister Fox, what's happened?

FOX. You — ! You rotten bastard — this is all your doing!

BYRON. What are you saying? Has he spoken? *(A gale of laughter offstage and the doors fly open. George III is wheeled on by Mrs. Crewe and the Duchess of Devonshire.)*

MRS. CREWE. Your Majesty, we mustn't excite ourselves.

GEORGE III. Laughing at me — what — the whole damn pack of them!

BYRON. Mister Fox?

DEVONSHIRE. Rose, do something.

MRS. CREWE. They didn't laugh, Your Majesty.

FOX. You poisoned him against me!

DEVONSHIRE. *(Seeing Byron.)* What are you doing here?

GEORGE III. *Gott in himmel, ich bin der König!*

DEVONSHIRE. You were to dine tonight with Lady Caroline.

BYRON. I told her to go home to her husband.

PRINNIE. *(Entering.)* There he is! There's my papa!

GEORGE III. Who's that?

BYRON. She shouldn't waste her time.

DEVONSHIRE. *(Seeing Prinnie.)* Good God, he's drunk.

MRS. CREWE. *(Barring Prinnie's way.)* I'm sorry, but I can't allow you to speak to him. You're in no fit state —

GEORGE III. What does he want from me?

BYRON. Mister Fox, please tell me — has he spoken?

MRS. CREWE. You're upsetting your father, sir.

BYRON. Mister Fox?

PRINNIE. *(Advancing.)* Does he not recognize his own flesh and blood? Out of my way! How dare you dictate whom I should marry? And look, there's the bitch-vulture herself — I'll

40

DEVONSHIRE. Prinnie, leave off!
GEORGE III. He's threatening me — my heart — !
MRS. CREWE. Your Majesty!
GEORGE III. I cannot breathe!
MRS. CREWE. Mister Fox — please help!
DEVONSHIRE. See what you've done?
GEORGE III. Spots! Large yellow spots before my eyes!
MRS. CREWE. *(In tears.)* I can't do it! I can't do this anymore!
DEVONSHIRE. *(To Prinnie.)* Stop it! Stop it! You're killing him!
MRS. CREWE. Your Majesty! Your Majesty!
GEORGE III. Infamy! Infamy! — My son's got it in f'me!

murder every one of you! I will obliterate you — and when I am king, no man shall stand above the rest to lord himself about as you have done. Liberty for all! Just like America! That's right — America! *(He begins marching about, miming the playing of a fife while chanting the melody of "Yankee Doodle Dandy.")*

(A massive deafening roar of voices from within, accompanied by stomping of feet. Sheridan appears as Fox had done, standing high within the House, speaking.)
SHERIDAN. Mister Speaker, Members of the House —
BYRON. Richard — no!
SHERIDAN. My learned colleague Mister Fox has warned you of the dangers in supporting these French rebels. I tell you that this revolution — this bloody act which has rended France asunder is not the child of hate; nor was it born from lack of moral principle, but from a God-inspired and superior love of human liberty. This love does rightfully reject that most accursed system of despotic government which has so crippled and corrupted human nature that it cannot recognize itself; a government that set at naught the property, the liberty, and lives of its subjects; a government that deals in extortion, dungeons, and tortures; a government which never hesitates to trample underfoot the slaves over which it rules. Would you have those slaves be so forever, or shall they not revolt and rise? I say, throw off your shackles, gentlemen, stand up with them and fight! For freedom, justice, and for liberty!
(Lights vanish on Sheridan as Pitt enters. He is very still.)

GEORGE III. Veronica!

FOX. Mister Pitt —

PITT. Mrs. Crewe, would you clear out the room. I'd like to be alone.

FOX. *(Advancing.)* Has the vote begun?

MRS. CREWE. Come along, Your Majesty. We should get you to bed. You're not well.

GEORGE III. I'm not going anywhere. I'm tired.

FOX. Mister Pitt?

PITT. *(Bellowing.)* Get out! All of you! Now!

GEORGE III. Why don't you get out, Veronica! Always pushing me around. Why don't you leave for a change?

PITT. I will not be barked at by a raving lunatic.

MRS. CREWE. Mister Pitt, this is the king. *(As Pitt speaks, a chant gathers in the House of Commons. The word "liberty." It grows louder and louder to the end of the act.)*

PITT. I don't care if Jesus Christ came in and sang me a South Sea Ballad — I've had enough! No, Mister Fox, the vote has not begun. I suggest, however, that you apply for the position of dogcatcher in the borough of Westminster, for you'll never sit as a representative in my House again! Listen to that! Sheridan has whipped the House into such a frenzy, there's talk of a referendum. They are paving the way to rebellion, Mister Fox, and I have you to thank for it. I will personally tear you both limb from limb — *(To the King.)* And as for you, you gibbering German inbreed — if it wasn't for me, you'd be locked up in some Yorkshire dairy sucking your big toe!

GEORGE III. *(Standing.)* Mister Pitt, you are addressing your king!

PITT. Sit down, old man. I've got a country to run! *(Chaos. Cries of "liberty" grow louder. Sheridan appears in a spot, triumphant, and the lights crash to darkness.)*

ACT TWO

Scene 1

An electrical storm. Thunder sounds, followed by loud knock-ing. The Duchess of Devonshire's apartments. The storm con-tinues to rage outside as Devonshire enters the dim room with candles. Her hair is down about her shoulders and she is dressed in a dressing gown. Byron follows close behind. He is wet with rain, pale and shaken.

DEVONSHIRE. What is it that is so important you must wake me in the middle of the night?

BYRON. You *could* sleep, couldn't you. Christ, if I'll ever sleep again —

DEVONSHIRE. Get to the point. I'm tired.

BYRON. *(Handing her a letter.)* There! My letter of resignation. I quit!

DEVONSHIRE. I'm in no humor for parlor games, Lord Byron.

BYRON. A simple night of drinking. A simple night of gin and forgetting at a squalid little inn until some pasty-faced boy appears, tugging at my sleeve. He shoves that in my face. At first I thought it was the drink because the words would not make sense, but then I see the signature. I ride like the devil. I knock. No one answers. I let myself indoors. The first thing that I notice is the stink. And papers everywhere. Upstairs I find him. A hairy rope swinging gen-tly from the beams. Shit staining his britches and his tongue as black as coal. I want to cut him down, but I cannot find a knife. I stand there on a chair and claw the hemp until my fingers bleed.

DEVONSHIRE. *(Reading.)* "This is the price of betrayal. Can you afford it? Charles James Fox." *(Pause.)* I don't see what this has to do with me.

BYRON. Get me a drink.

DEVONSHIRE. This is not my doing. Come back tomorrow. We'll buy you some new clothes. Breed cultivation in the man. Get you a haircut.

BYRON. This is not a game, woman! Your intrigues and your plots — they cost men's lives!

DEVONSHIRE. I am sorry the Lord Byron had an unfortunate experience. You should have ignored this note. *(Tearing it up.)* You should have dined with Lady Caroline as I arranged. The woman is in love with you.

BYRON. The woman is a lunatic and so are you if you imagine I'll continue this deception. To hell with all your plans! Richard Sheridan is my friend! I will not end my days swinging in some attic because I betrayed a friend.

DEVONSHIRE. I hope you do not think now you're a success that you're above the law. There's only one thing people cherish more than building idols for themselves, and that's to tear them down.

BYRON. I am waiting for that drink.

DEVONSHIRE. Two months ago I could have gone to the committee and told them all about those rough boys you take home with you and no one would have blinked. You were nothing then. Now you have a name they can't wait to drink your blood. You'd make lovely scandal fodder. You see, all success really means is now you're hated more than you ever were before.

BYRON. You cannot frighten me. I will not do your bidding.

DEVONSHIRE. I saved your reputation, sir. That's as good as save your life. I believe I've earned some gratitude.

BYRON. You net twenty-five percent off every copy of my book. That's more than gratitude — it's exploitation.

DEVONSHIRE. How dare you show me such contempt?

BYRON. I learned the art from you.

DEVONSHIRE. You say that Sheridan is your friend. Would he remain your friend, I wonder, if he knew how you've deceived him?

BYRON. What?

DEVONSHIRE. I would inform on you with pleasure, sir. What would he say, I wonder, if he knew that he'd embraced a serpent to his heart?

BYRON. My God, you are a monster! I brought you seven of those

44

letters. Even when I knew that I was doing wrong, I still delivered them. I stole, I forged, I lied — what more do you want from me?

DEVONSHIRE. The prince is to be married and I want it stopped. Do what you must, but see it done.

BYRON. I cannot get the sight of him out of my mind. His eyes bulging from his head, staring at me as his body swung so gently.

DEVONSHIRE. *(Handing a glass.)* Here's your drink. Finish it and let yourself out. And no more talk of resignation. You'll do as you are told. *(Mrs. Crewe steps out of the shadows, naked, rubbing her eyes.)*

MRS. CREWE. I heard voices. Where did you go? Oh.

DEVONSHIRE. Go back to bed.

BYRON. What have we here?

DEVONSHIRE. Go back. Go back!

MRS. CREWE. I — I'm sorry, I didn't know —

DEVONSHIRE. Go back! *(Byron begins to laugh as Mrs. Crewe exits, running and crying.)*

BYRON. *(Laughing.)* Your Grace — you dark horse, you.

DEVONSHIRE. This isn't what you think.

BYRON. I think it's now a question of who points the finger first.

DEVONSHIRE. You dare to threaten me? Get out of my house! *(Byron drains his drink and holds out the glass.)*

BYRON. More! *(Deafening thunder. Blackout.)*

Scene 2

The changing room at the Drury Lane Theatre. The long table is cleared, except for a deck of cards laid out for solitaire. Sheridan sits, his wig at his side, a towel draped over his head. His feet soak in a basin of hot water. Hopkins enters carrying a stack of scripts on top of which rests a prop crown.

HOPKINS. Miss Robinson is out again. This makes it five days in a row.

SHERIDAN. *(Sneezes.)* I hope every time I sneeze she feels a pain right in her heart. What's all this then?

HOPKINS. You wanted to see the crown we used last year for *Tamburlaine*.

SHERIDAN. Yes, that'll do nicely. See if it fits Mister Kemble for *Lear*. I caught cold outside her window calling out her name all night. It rained.

HOPKINS. And these are the last of the scripts from the cellar. I was using them to prop up the throne for the Scottish play.

SHERIDAN. *(Flipping through them.)* *Confessions of a Chambermaid, The Loves of Lancelot* — A pitiful waste of perfectly good paper. I know she was at home. I saw a light behind the shutters.

HOPKINS. *A Trip to Scarborough* by Richard Brin ... Sir, this is one of yours! Why not revive it?

SHERIDAN. Better still — maybe I can pass it off as new. She wanted a new play. She'd never know the difference, would she?

HOPKINS. *(Leafing through the script.)* Actually, it appears she played in it the first time round.

SHERIDAN. Oh, what's the use. Planning a theatre season is like planning your own funeral — who gives a toss as long as its simple, inexpensive, and draws an enormous crowd.

HOPKINS. Speaking of funerals, sir. You asked me to check the newspapers. It's Saturday at three.

SHERIDAN. *(Returning to his game of solitaire.)* Thank you, Hopkins.

HOPKINS. Sir? Why did Mister Fox hang himself? They say you betrayed him by voting against the king.

SHERIDAN. Do they. And what do you think?

HOPKINS. I don't think, sir. I'm a working man. I only listen.

SHERIDAN. They got it backwards. He betrayed the party. And if my oration in the House had less to do with any grand beliefs than my desire to rub his face in it — so be it.

HOPKINS. But wasn't Mister Fox your friend?

SHERIDAN. He was a bloody traitor. I don't feel guilty and don't see why I should. I had nothing to do with it. Besides, Pitt has won his vote, thanks to some veiled threats he delivered to the House. Since then he's redoubled his efforts to purge the world of all he sees as immoral and unfit.

HOPKINS. Does that mean there's to be no revolt then?

SHERIDAN. Alas, no. Everything's revolting enough as it is. *(Pitt enters at the back, unseen.)*

HOPKINS. But if people know they have a chance for something better in their lives —

SHERIDAN. I'll put it this way, boy: are you happy in your work here?

HOPKINS. Happy? I don't know that I rightly think like that. I do what needs doing and you pay me on occasion.

SHERIDAN. You see? There are more things in heaven and earth than are dreamt of on our little stage.

HOPKINS. Sir?

PITT. *Hamlet. (Sheridan and Hopkins turn.)* Forgive me. I didn't mean to interrupt. Only the stage door was open and there was no one there.

SHERIDAN. Hopkins, will you go and lock that door for God's sake. *(Hopkins exits. Pitt advances slowly, looking about with curiosity.)*

PITT. I took the liberty of nosing around a bit. Amateur curiosity. It's amazing the things you have around. Swords, armor — even a crown! Now that is quite a find. Or is that one of your personal items? *(Pause. He looks up at the ceiling.)* Take this contraption in the ceiling — that looks interesting. What is it? A device of some sort?

SHERIDAN. Yes.

PITT. I see. So if you're standing up on stage and someone wants to, say, get rid of you, they'd only have to open up that door and — whoosh!

SHERIDAN. *(Coldly.)* Whoosh.

PITT. How ingenious. Does it have a name? I'm very keen on the names of things. The professional vocabulary.

SHERIDAN. It's called the trap.

PITT. And the room below it — here?

SHERIDAN. We call it Hell.

PITT. *(Looking up.)* Yes, I like that very much.

SHERIDAN. Would you care to try it out? *(Pitt smiles. Silence.)* What are you doing in my theatre, Mister Pitt? Shouldn't you be out hanging prostitutes or other honest working folk?

PITT. People underestimate the theatre — its political potential. The Drury Lane — well, it's more than a theatre; it is history cast in stone. But then there's your financial difficulties. It seemed like the perfect opportunity. Why buy a ticket for one play when I can purchase a controlling interest in the theatre itself. And so I did. To the exact tune of seventy-five percent of the shares.

SHERIDAN. You what? That's impossible. Those shares are not for sale. They're part of the Garrick estate.

PITT. And what a business it was having my lawyers take care of it all. The price of the insurance alone is enough to ruin a man.

SHERIDAN. You bought out three-quarters of my theatre?

PITT. It's so important for government to get involved in the arts, don't you think? *(Pause.)* I must say, I do admire that crown. Lovely craftsmanship. Why don't you put it on? Let me see what it looks like worn. *(Pitt holds out the crown to Sheridan.)*

SHERIDAN. Go to hell.

PITT. Now, now. Is that any way to speak to a partner? I insist. *(Stern.)* Put it on. *(Sheridan takes the crown and places it on his head.)* That's lovely. You ought to wear it more often. *(Leans in.)* I'm going to ruin you, Sheridan. And what's more, I'm going to enjoy it. *(Exiting.)* Please don't get up; I'll see myself out. *(Pitt leaves whistling. Sheridan removes the crown.)*

SHERIDAN. *(Bellowing.)* Hopkins! *(Hopkins enters.)* Don't you ever let that man down here again! Get me some paper and ink!

HOPKINS. Sir?

SHERIDAN. Paper and ink! Stop gawping at me, lad!

HOPKINS. Are you going to write, sir?

SHERIDAN. I may be out of practice, but I'm not yet dead!

HOPKINS. *(Overjoyed.)* Yes, sir! *(Hopkins runs off excitedly.)*

SHERIDAN. And get me my shoes! I've been soaking so long, my toes have turned to figs!

HOPKINS. *(Rushing on with paper and ink.)* Right away, sir! *(Hopkins exits again, running. Sheridan begins tapping his quill in the ink.)*

SHERIDAN. The poxy snake thinks he can best me like that? Underestimate it's potential? I'll show him potential — him and his damn committee! — I'll denounce him from the rooftops! — I'll — I'll — *(Calling.)* Shoes, boy! *(Turning back to the page.)* Now then — *(Sheridan stares at the paper, unable to move. Finally, he writes a few words in a furious frenzy. He sits back, reads them over, adds a line. Perdita appears, carrying a small dress case. They see each other and stop. An uncomfortable silence.)* You're late. *(Pause.)* Going somewhere?

PERDITA. I haven't been feeling well. I thought perhaps a few days in the country might do me good. I've just come to get a few of my things.

SHERIDAN. You should have sent a note round to let us know your plans.

PERDITA. I did. Didn't Hopkins —

SHERIDAN. I meant a more personal — never mind.

PERDITA. *(Pause. Passing by him.)* Excuse me. *(Begins folding dresses into her dress case.)*

SHERIDAN. I came by your home. Several times. I knocked. Called your name.

PERDITA. *(Silence.)* Did you.

SHERIDAN. I think I broke a window. I don't remember.

PERDITA. I see.

SHERIDAN. I — I've missed you. *(Silence.)* Did you hear what I said?

PERDITA. Yes.

SHERIDAN. *(Pause.)* Dammit — I'm lost without you, Perdie. I need you with me. You must tell me what I've done — if I have hurt you in some way —

PERDITA. *(Facing him.)* Richard, I don't think it's a good idea for me to continue working here. Together. For us to — I've been offered a contract with Covent Garden. I've told them I'm going to take it.

SHERIDAN. *(Silence. Slightly dazed.)* I see. That's it then, is it?

PERDITA. It's important you know my decision had nothing to do with you.

SHERIDAN. That's supposed to make me feel better?

PERDITA. That isn't what I mean.

SHERIDAN. Fidelity strikes again.

PERDITA. Listen, they've offered me a choice of parts. I thought perhaps I could help you. I thought I might suggest one of yours. *School for Scandal* or *The Scheming Lieutenant.*

SHERIDAN. Is there a man behind this?

PERDITA. *(Laughing.)* You'd like that.

SHERIDAN. Who is he?

PERDITA. There's no one.

SHERIDAN. Of course, but what's his name?

PERDITA. I'm trying to help you, Richard.

SHERIDAN. Bugger your help! I don't want your fucking charity. I'll give you choice of parts. For God's sake, you can play Hamlet for all I care! Only tell me, what have I done? Why are you doing this to me?

PERDITA. Doing to you? This isn't about you, Richard. It's about me. I'm doing to me. I'm doing some good to me for a change. I'm dragging myself out of here because I've had enough. I won't grieve for your life before it's over. I won't sit by and watch you disintegrate before my eyes.

SHERIDAN. I supported your damn rebels.

PERDITA. Yes, and where's my fucking play? You promised me a play, Richard! You think I wanted you to support those lousy Jacobins for nothing? I hoped you'd get inspired and write me something new — something current — something that spoke to hearts and minds. Something to get me noticed for a change! I won't be young forever, Richard, and once that's gone, where's my career? Playing mothers? Nurses? End up like Miss Pope? Not on your bloody life, I won't!

SHERIDAN. All this — ? For a play — ?

PERDITA. It's how I live! Now get out of my way. *(She continues to pack.)*

SHERIDAN. *(Pause.)* Those dresses are theatre property.

PERDITA. Consider them compensation for all the back pay you owe.

SHERIDAN. You're nothing but a vampire. All this — everything I've tried to do — *(Miss Pope enters with Hopkins following.)*

HOPKINS. No — Miss Pope, he isn't here! You mustn't —

MISS POPE. Would you look who's finally shown his ugly face!

HOPKINS. I tried to stop her, sir.

MISS POPE. You're not getting away this time, Mister S. It's been months since I've seen hide or hair of you and I want my money, understand? Money. It's high time you began appreciating my talents round here.

SHERIDAN. Yes, of course. And what is it you do?

MISS POPE. Why, of all the cheek! I make your stinking words worth listening to, that's what I do! I'm the reason people come to hear your plays!

SHERIDAN. Oh, I see. And all this time I've blamed myself for that.

MISS POPE. *(Noticing Perdita.)* And look who else the cat dragged in — if it isn't the bloody Queen of Sheba! Is she here to work or just on a social visit? I imagine now you've lost that reelection of yours, Mister S., you'll want to sort things out round here.

SHERIDAN. That's a very good idea, Miss Pope. I'll start with you. You're fired.

MISS POPE. What?

SHERIDAN. *(Tossing a pouch of coins.)* There's your money, now shut your face. Hopkins, get this blithering cow out of my sight!

MISS POPE. *(As Hopkins ushers her to the door.)* But — but you can't! I'll have you for this! You wait and see, I'll — I'll — I'll — *(Hopkins closes the door on Miss Pope. Sheridan picks up the crown.)*

SHERIDAN. What's this doing here?

HOPKINS. That's Lear's crown for Mister Kemble. Are you all right, sir?

SHERIDAN. We can't use this. We had it last year for *Tamburlaine* — Take it away.

HOPKINS. But, sir, you said —

SHERIDAN. Are you going to argue with me, boy?

HOPKINS. I'm only trying to say that —

SHERIDAN. Good — you're fired as well! *(Sheridan puts the crown on Hopkins and shoves him out the door.)* Are you still here?

PERDITA. *(Offering her hand.)* It was a pleasure working with you, Mister Sheridan.

SHERIDAN. Oh, what a mind-boggling gesture! Did it ever occur to you, my dear, that I didn't write your fucking play because you're just not bloody good enough? *(Perdita gathers her bags and exits as Sheridan calls after her.)* You're nothing! The whole stinking lot of you! You've got no heart! You're just another actress — a dressmaker's dummy with a voice! Millions more where you came from! You're nothing! Nothing! *(Loud hoofbeats. Thunder. Heavy rain.)*

Scene 3

A split scene: the Duchess of Devonshire's writing closet and the drawing room of Mrs. Maria Fitzherbert's house. The decor of the drawing room is tasteless but expensive. A table with a decanter of wine. The storm rages outside. Devonshire is writing a letter.

DEVONSHIRE. To the Right Honorable Richard Sheridan — Dear Sir — *(Drunken singing can be heard offstage.)* When one discovers an injustice, it is our duty to defend the innocent. When the injustice is betrayal, it becomes a moral imperative. *(Sheridan and Byron enter, leading a singing Irish priest between them. This is Father Rammage. He is small, bespectacled, and very drunk. The three are rain-soaked.)*

SHERIDAN. Shut your gob and watch your step, you're dripping everywhere! *(To Byron.)* Where in hell did you find this man?

BYRON. Mrs. O'Malley's winery. More reliable than a Catholic church.

SHERIDAN. What do you mean, Catholic? This man's a priest? *(Laughing.)* Oh, good God, George, you are one in a million!

BYRON. What's so amusing? *(Seeing Rammage reach for the wine.)* Don't you fucking touch that!

RAMMAGE. *(Drinking.)* The blood of Christ, my son. *Pax vobiscum* and down the hatch.

DEVONSHIRE. To my mind, few offenses reach the rank and heinous depths of full iniquity as that of the betrayal of a friend.

SHERIDAN. We can't give him a priest — have you lost your mind?

BYRON. The bride is Catholic. You do want them married, don't you?

DEVONSHIRE. Sadly, it falls to me to be the one informing you —

BYRON. I was only trying to help.

DEVONSHIRE. — You are the victim of this crime. *(Rammage begins to sneeze, wiping his nose on his sleeve.)*

SHERIDAN. Well then help me get him out of those wet things before we have a *dead* priest on our hands.

DEVONSHIRE. The perpetrator of this offense is none other than the young man in your company, the Lord Byron. He is no friend of yours, but a traitor, an informer, and betrayer of your trust. *(Sheridan and Byron begin undressing Rammage.)*

RAMMAGE. Now wait a moment, lads — what sort of ceremony is this?

SHERIDAN. Be still. It's for your own good.

RAMMAGE. *(Giggling.)* That's what we tell the choirboys when we make them castrati.

DEVONSHIRE. — I only hope that I am warning you in time.

BYRON. *(Pulling off Rammage's shoe.)* Off with the right one —

SHERIDAN. *(Pulling off the other shoe.)* Off with the left one —

RAMMAGE. *(Giggling.)* We say that too!

DEVONSHIRE. — Signed — With humblest respect — A friend. *(Prinnie rushes on, anxious, dressed in full finery. Lights vanish on Devonshire.)*

PRINNIE. Oh, thank God it's you! Sherry, I've been frantic. Every time I hear the sound of hoofbeats, I think it's my father coming to stop the whole thing. *(Prinnie sees Rammage, who stands stripped to the waist and barefoot.)* Why is there a naked man in this room?

SHERIDAN. It's called the best we could find.

RAMMAGE. *(Sign of the cross.)* In nomine Patris et Filii and how d'you do.

PRINNIE. Are you purposefully trying to destroy me? And who the devil is that?

SHERIDAN. This is my good friend George. George, may I introduce George?

PRINNIE. I told you, Sherry — no outsiders.

SHERIDAN. You can trust him, sir. He's probably the only trustworthy man in London.

RAMMAGE. *(Approaching.)* And my name is Father Rammage —

PRINNIE. Get this creature dressed and on his way!

RAMMAGE. Wait a minute! I know you! By all the saints —

PRINNIE. How could you do this to me, Sherry — today, of all days?

RAMMAGE. You're Prince George! *(Falls to his knees.)* Long live Prince George!

PRINNIE. The woman I love is upstairs waiting and you bring me *this?* I promised her the perfect wedding —

BYRON. All the more reason to use the priest, Your Highness. Without a priest, your Catholic bride would not be seen as truly married, at least in the eyes of her God.

RAMMAGE. May I say what an honor this is —

PRINNIE. Have you any comprehension of the terrors I've been facing? The number of times I've had to assuage her fears? I entrust you with one simple little task and you louse it up — as per usual, I might add!

RAMMAGE. Your Majesty is like a star in the firmament of heaven —

SHERIDAN. *(Overlapping.)* As per usual? What the hell do you mean by —

BYRON. *(Overlapping.)* He's nervous, Richard. Let it go.

PRINNIE. *(Overlapping.)* You think you're very clever — well, I've had it up to here with your bloody Irish ways. *(A bell rings off. Prinnie squeals in fright.)*

SHERIDAN. What was that?

BYRON. *(Pause.)* There's someone at the door.

PRINNIE. It's my father! I know it's my father! He's followed you here with his men to put a stop to the service. This is all your bloody fault! Well don't just stand there — *do* something!

SHERIDAN. What do you want *me* to do?

PRINNIE. Hide me, answer it, kill them — anything!

SHERIDAN. *(Exiting.)* I'll see who it is.

PRINNIE. Oh, this is the end! — The *end!* I can feel it! — and after everything I've prayed for —

RAMMAGE. God hears all our prayers, my son.

PRINNIE. Oh, do shut up.

BYRON. You'd better hide, Your Majesty. In case —

PRINNIE. Yes — yes — hide — hide! — Under the table! Quick!

(The three men hide under the table. Rammage emerges briefly to take the bottle of wine. Sheridan reenters slowly, turning a sealed letter over

in his hands. Byron emerges, followed by Prinnie.)

BYRON. Well?

SHERIDAN. *(Perplexed.)* Only a woman. In a mask. With a letter.

PRINNIE. A letter? It must be for Maria. Give it to me, I'll take it up to her.

SHERIDAN. — Addressed to me.

PRINNIE. To you? *(Sheridan shows him the letter.)* But why would — ?

BYRON. Did she leave her name?

SHERIDAN. No, but she said it was important that I read it in your presence.

BYRON. My — ?

PRINNIE. *(Nervously.)* I don't like this. I don't like this at all.

BYRON. Perhaps I should have a look at that.

SHERIDAN. Whatever for?

PRINNIE. How would anyone know you're here? You told someone, didn't you? Who was it?

SHERIDAN. For God's sake, I didn't tell a soul!

PRINNIE. *(Pointing at Byron.)* You told *him!* Well, go on — open it!

BYRON. *(Desperate.)* Richard, no! I mean — if this is some ploy to stop the wedding — we should ignore it. We should proceed as if nothing's happened.

SHERIDAN. That's ridiculous.

BYRON. All right — all right — but first lets drink a toast! To the health of the bride and groom — *(Quickly hands out glasses.)* — and to the many years of joy ahead — now where's the bloody wine? (Byron spots Rammage under the table and kicks him.)*

RAMMAGE. *(Emerging.)* Dearly beloved, we are gathered here in the sight of God —

BYRON. Not yet! Father, would you do the honors? Richard, read it later!

RAMMAGE. You're sure you're not Irish, m'boyo? *(As Rammage goes to fill Sheridan's glass, Byron nudges him, causing him to spill the wine all over the letter.)*

SHERIDAN. Christ, mind what you're doing! Clumsy drunken oaf!

BYRON. *(Taking the wet letter.)* Let me dry that for you.

RAMMAGE. My apologies, sir — I was only trying to —

PRINNIE. You did that on purpose!

BYRON. What?

PRINNIE. You pushed him! I saw you!

SHERIDAN. Can you make out a name? Anything at all?

BYRON. I'm afraid it's no use. Completely ruined.

PRINNIE. There's something going on here, I can tell. You know something about that letter.

BYRON. Who, me? That's absurd.

SHERIDAN. George?

BYRON. I don't know what he means.

PRINNIE. I don't believe him.

SHERIDAN. If he says he doesn't know, sir, then he doesn't know.

PRINNIE. He's lying!

SHERIDAN. He'd never lie to me.

BYRON. Sir, we came here to ensure your wedding passed without incident. Now shall we bring down the bride and proceed with the service?

PRINNIE. Don't you patronize me! Why, I'll have you whipped for — for — I'll find a bloody reason and have you whipped for it. Who do you think you are?

SHERIDAN. Sir, he is my friend and I will not stand to have you speak to him like this. Whatever your delusions are, you will kindly show him the courtesy that he deserves.

PRINNIE. Delusions? Pish! The only thing I'll show him is the door!

SHERIDAN. Sir —

PRINNIE. And don't you lecture me! This whole disaster's your fault and well you know it!

SHERIDAN. Right. Come on, George, we're going.

PRINNIE. What? Are you out of your mind?

SHERIDAN. I don't need to stand here and be insulted.

BYRON. Richard, don't. This isn't necessary.

PRINNIE. I did not insult you; I insulted him.

SHERIDAN. Insult my friend, sir, and you've insulted me.

BYRON. Gentlemen — please — the wedding —

SHERIDAN. George, let's go.

PRINNIE. Dammit, I am your prince! You will stay and you will do as you are told!

SHERIDAN. I'm not your whipping boy. I won't be spoken to like that.

BYRON. Richard, please — let's not —

PRINNIE. Like what? I'll speak howe'er I please!

BYRON. He's got a touch of cold. He doesn't mean it, sir.

PRINNIE. And you keep out of this, you greasy little man!

SHERIDAN. When I think of everything I've done for you — the countless women I've procured so you'd have someone to tuck up with for the night. When I think of the time and the expense —

BYRON. Richard, don't!

SHERIDAN. — And all for what?

PRINNIE. Now you look here — !

SHERIDAN. Why do I do it? What obscene compulsion so impels me to rush about as young Prince George's pimp and messenger?

PRINNIE. Sheridan, I'm warning you!

SHERIDAN. I'll tell you, shall I? Because one sunny day five years ago, the puffed-up Prince of Wales invested some money in my theatre. Five years ago and not a penny since! Does it ever occur to you in that empty gilded cage you call a brain that some mere mortals have to struggle to get by? That life, for some, is not served up on a silver charger for a treat?

PRINNIE. You ungrateful Irish bastard!

SHERIDAN. You stomp through life like a bloody great bull —

PRINNIE. — And to think I trusted you!

SHERIDAN. — Like a nasty spoiled child —

PRINNIE. — I should have known!

SHERIDAN. Christ, but I resent you — !

PRINNIE. Now we see the man for what he is! Maria had suspicions, and I said no, but she was right! You've done nothing but betray me all this time!

SHERIDAN. Me? Betraying you?

PRINNIE. Oh don't you dare play coy! You think we'd never guess what you'd been doing with our letters?

BYRON. I think we should go now, Richard.

SHERIDAN. What about your stinking letters?

PRINNIE. You pose yourself as loyal — you're the biggest Judas yet!

BYRON.   Gentlemen, enough! We've all said things that we regret —

SHERIDAN. No! He'll tell me what he means!

PRINNIE. As if you didn't know!

BYRON. We really ought to leave.

PRINNIE.   Giving them to that she-wolf, that gorgon, the Duchess of Devonshire.

BYRON. Richard, I'm begging you —

SHERIDAN. What complete and utter rubbish! I never showed your letters to a soul. The only person I ever gave them to was — *(He looks at Byron.)*

BYRON. *(Pause.)* Richard, take your coat. Please take it and let's go. It isn't what you think. I can explain —

PRINNIE. I never want to see you again. I never want to hear your voice or speak your name! You're dead to me! You're dead! *(Prinnie exits. A long silence.)*

RAMMAGE. Does this mean the wedding's off? *(And Rammage collapses unconscious to the ground.)*

BYRON. You've got to let me explain, Richard. It wasn't done by choice. She made me do it. She forced my hand. She blackmailed me.

SHERIDAN. How does one blackmail the devil?

BYRON. What can I say to apologize? Richard, look at me! I told her I wouldn't do it. I told her I resign. Richard Sheridan is my friend, I said, I will not stand for this. I would never — that's why I came here tonight — to see the wedding through. To throw it in her face and put things right. The number of times I wanted to tell you — to warn you — each time you called me friend, my heart would — look at me! That day you spoke in Parliament, I knew! I knew that all the apathy was but a show and that you still believed! Good God, it tore my heart, but you would not be stopped. Silver-tongued Sheridan! I was so proud of you. Look at me. Don't do this! Say something!

SHERIDAN. You're a deceitful little cripple and I hope you die alone.

BYRON. *(Going to him.)* Richard, you're my friend — *(Sheridan erupts in a deafening howl, swinging his fists. Byron falls backwards.*

Sheridan lifts a chair at him, but stops. He throws it against a wall. Byron rushes off. Sheridan tries to regain himself. He can't. The loud banging of a gavel —)

Scene 4

The Old Bailey. A long table. Many papers. Justice McKeye is seated, dressed in formal judicial robes, holding an ear trumpet. Pitt stands. The Duchess of Devonshire stands opposite.

PITT. M'lud, if the accused will not answer the question, I will request she be cited for contempt in addition to her stated charges.

McKEYE. You'll have to speak up, I —

PITT. Contempt!

DEVONSHIRE. You have asked me to confess but you have not read my charges. Of what am I accused?

McKEYE. Your Grace, you are a privileged defendant. Less fortunate women have been put in the stocks or to hard labor for offenses such as yours. Our learned Mister Pitt is offering you the courtesy of a trial. I urge you to take advantage of this opportunity.

DEVONSHIRE. How can I, m'lud, when I do not know the charge?

PITT. You know very well the charge. You are accused of being unchaste. Will you confess?

DEVONSHIRE. Unchaste? On what ground?

PITT. Common decency prevents me naming it.

DEVONSHIRE. If you cannot name the crime, I cannot confess to it.

PITT. Dammit, woman! It is for your own good!

DEVONSHIRE. Who is it accuses me? I demand to know.

PITT. The informant remains anonymous.

DEVONSHIRE. And I am innocent.

PITT. With your permission, m'lud, I wish to submit into evidence in this case the signed confession of Mrs. Rose Crewe.

DEVONSHIRE. Inadmissible!

McKEYE. Who? *(Pitt hands Justice McKeye several papers.)* Ah yes. *(Banging his gavel.)* Silence!

DEVONSHIRE. That document was signed under duress. It isn't worth the paper it's printed on.

McKEYE. *(Staring at Devonshire blankly.)* What did she say?

DEVONSHIRE. M'lud, she was beaten. She was put in stocks and men threw rocks at her face. Your men did this! I will not recognize the authority of this committee!

PITT. *(Referring to the papers.)* M'lud?

McKEYE. *(Handing Pitt the papers.)* Yes, very good. Evidence accepted.

PITT. You are familiar with this document, Your Grace? *(Silence.)* Are you familiar with the person who put her signature to this document, the late Mrs. Rose Crewe? *(Silence.)* Shall I read you this document, Your Grace? *(The Duchess of Devonshire weeps silently.)* "I, the undersigned, Mrs. Rose Crewe, do humbly submit to the committee the following instances as proof of my moral degeneracy and that of — "

DEVONSHIRE. Stop!

PITT. Have you reconsidered your position regarding this matter, Your Grace?

DEVONSHIRE. Yes.

PITT. Do you confess to the charges brought against you by this committee?

DEVONSHIRE. Yes.

PITT. Do you admit to being unchaste, morally degenerate, and a threat to the common decency of this land?

DEVONSHIRE. Yes.

PITT. Are you prepared to sign a statement to this effect and accept the sovereignty of this committee in passing judgment?

DEVONSHIRE. Yes.

PITT. M'lud?

McKEYE. Charlotte Teverton, Duchess of Devonshire, you have pled guilty before this committee to all charges leveled against you. In order to consider judgment, the court would like your cooperation in supplying us with the names of other persons of questionable character. Should you comply and assist us in this way, the court will show considered leniency during sentencing. Charlotte Teverton, do you wish to furnish us with information of this kind?

DEVONSHIRE. I wish to submit the name of George Gordon, the Lord Byron.

PITT. The court notes the compliance and cooperation of the accused. Be you prepared to receive sentence. *(Pitt writes Byron's name down in a book.)*

McKEYE. Charlotte Teverton, the sentence of this committee is that all holdings, properties, and investments belonging to you in name, title, or deed be transferred and collected by the state. Thank you for your cooperation in this matter. You are free to go. *(Justice McKeye bangs his gavel. Devonshire's mouth opens in a soundless cry. She faints.)*

Scene 5

The sounds of a blaze. People shouting "Fire!" A dim red light far offstage. Smoke pours onto the stage. People rush from the smoke and some into it. A light rises on Sheridan sitting at a small table outside The Golden Lamb Public House. In front of him is a carafe of wine, half empty.

SHERIDAN. Every Saturday night, after final curtain, we'd collect the candle ends — the hardened pools of wax on floors — the long and stiffened streams on curtains would be scraped off in a bucket — and then laughing, giddy, young, and thinking we knew better than the best of them, we'd run the buckets down the mills and have them melted into new ones. Always at four in the morning when the dew came — always when the long and lonely shadows played across the empty cobbled streets — always waking the candlemakers from sleep or lovemaking. Now the seat cushions — the curtains — the creaking old wardrobes — corsets and bonnets and mirrors and papers — a floorboard in the hall David Garrick carved his name on

— the last time I ever made love to you was on a stairway which is now burning. The candles are melted, Eliza. All the wax is scattered. *(He is still. Byron runs on, soot on his face, breathless.)*

BYRON. I came as soon as I heard. All across town there's an enormous black cloud. People look up and can't see the sky. Thank God you're not hurt. For a moment I thought — I don't know what I thought. There's men trying to rescue the furniture, but they say two have already choked to death on smoke. *(Catches his breath.)* What the hell are you doing?

SHERIDAN. Cannot a man have a drink by his own fireside?

BYRON. It's all gone. Don't you understand? The theatre is lost. They're saying that it's arson. They've made arrests.

SHERIDAN. They'll never get him.

BYRON. Do you know who it is? Richard, if you do, you must report them.

SHERIDAN. *(Laughing.)* To whom? The police? Mister Pitt? Don't be daft.

BYRON. You don't mean he's involved. You can't be serious.

SHERIDAN. At first I thought you might have done it. But there is no poetry to be had in the burning of a theatre. You're more the sort to brain a man with the jawbone of an ass.

BYRON. Richard, I've come to help. Can't we see beyond that? I still consider you my friend.

SHERIDAN. I have but one friend in this world — the vintner of this wine. Alas, he has betrayed me too, for I am stone-cold sober.

BYRON. How can you sit here drinking while your theatre burns?

SHERIDAN. Oh, little man, I've dreamt about this day. Every trace of the past, every connection to memory, disappearing in a puff of smoke. I give a toast and say good riddance. Only pity is you weren't inside.

BYRON. I want you to forgive me, Richard. I tell you, I will not move from this spot until you do.

SHERIDAN. You are standing in my view.

BYRON. Stop it! Stop playing these games and speak to me as a man. Tell me what to do, what to say, but I will not be dismissed!

SHERIDAN. You're not a man. You're nothing but a whore. A spoiled, arrogant hypocrite without a sense of shame. Ah, but he has ideals! See him as he sits atop his ivory tower casting pearls of wisdom on the swine below, instructing all and sundry on the troubles of the world; to find its fault, to lay the blame, he points his finger at the other man and with a haughty sneer accuses him of not being all he should. Ideals are the curse of the privileged class!

BYRON. At least I try! At least I strive!

SHERIDAN. You do nothing but manipulate.

BYRON. Perhaps I have, and I was wrong. Yes, I made a horrible mistake and I was wrong. How else can I apologize? For all my faults, though, is it wrong for me to look for some perfection in this world? To hope that other hearts may search for goodness and for truth that I find lacking in my own small soul? I still believe in that!

SHERIDAN. Keep talking, you might yet convince yourself. You say you have belief? So what? What right have you to put me on a pedestal when you've no idea as to who I am? You've never had to fight, you've never had to sweat to eat. As soon as there's a threat, you sell your soul to save your skin. Where's your belief when it's your comfort, cash, and reputation that mean more to you than life?

BYRON. Perhaps it's you who put me on a pedestal. Perhaps I awoke those ideals in you and now you fear they're shattered. Could it be you're angry now for seeing all my faults? Perhaps it's you who really do believe.

SHERIDAN. Piss off.

BYRON. How dare you lecture me on loyalty? You turned your back on Charlie Fox when that man needed you the most —

SHERIDAN. No!

BYRON. Don't make the same mistake again! I beg you —

SHERIDAN. No!

BYRON. Mister Pitt has put out a subpoena for me to appear before his committee. Please, Richard — as a weak, imperfect, frightened friend, I ask you for your help.

SHERIDAN. *(A toast; a laugh.)* Now that is poetic justice. I hope he breaks you, George. I hope he rubs your face in shit.

BYRON. *(Pause.)* I can't believe you would say such a thing.

SHERIDAN. Why don't you go home and write a poem about it. *(Byron steps back, staring at Sheridan. He turns and exits as Sheridan pours another drink. He holds it up in a toast to the fire.)* Burn — burn, you bastard! Give me surfeit of your smoke and choke the past in ash. I defy remembrance! *(He drinks. Lights rise on George III in his wheelchair. Pitt stands nearby. Prinnie sits at a distance, weeping silently.)*

GEORGE III. Look, Veronica. Another sunset.

PITT. That's a fire, your majesty. The Drury Lane is burning.

GEORGE III. That is sad, no?

PITT. It was a bad investment. Putting money into a theatre is an utter waste. I must find a better way to break that man.

GEORGE III. Oh, there is something in me that feels very tired. It wasn't right of me. It wasn't right to marry him to that — what —

PITT. Princess Caroline of Brunswick.

PRINNIE. *(Sobbing.)* She's a cow!

GEORGE III. I have a feeling he does not love her. Mind you, she is a terrifically ugly woman.

PITT. It was a diplomatic allegiance. Love does not enter into it.

GEORGE III. I've known some ugly women in my time — but her! *Unglaublich — ja — eine unglaubliche frau.* Will he ever forgive me?

PITT. *(To Prinnie.)* You forgive your father, don't you?

PRINNIE. Never! May he rot in hell!

GEORGE III. It wasn't right.

PITT. Breaking a man of his convictions is a sign of authority, Your Highness. He has learned to respect you now.

GEORGE III. Has he? I don't know. What is respect without love? You are very intelligent, Veronica. But you have no heart. Oh dear.

PITT. Your Majesty?

GEORGE III. I think — *ja* — I think I am going to die now.

PITT. Nonsense. You have years left, Your Majesty. Your Majesty? *(Pitt looks at the King. He is dead. Prinnie stops crying and approaches.)*

PRINNIE. Is he — ?

PITT. *(Covering the King's face.)* So it seems.

PRINNIE. 'Struth! *(Silence.)* But he can't be! I'm not ready! How am I — what am I — after all these years, I'm finally to be —

PITT. King, Your Majesty.

PRINNIE. *(Pause.)* Mister Pitt, what do I do? You must help me, sir.

PITT. You could always start a war.

PRINNIE. Ah. Yes. Yes. What?

PITT. War. It's good for the morale. You might try the French.

This Napoleon chap.

PRINNIE. I see. Right. I'll talk to Admiral Nelson.

PITT. First you might want to tell the queen, your wife.

PRINNIE. What? Oh, yes! Yes. Thank you, Mister Pitt. Thank you. *(Exiting.)* Caroline! My own! Dearest! We're going to have a war! *(As the King vanishes into darkness, Pitt steps down into —)*

Scene 6

Debtor's prison. Squalor. Filth. Distantly, a woman hums a lullaby. Dogs bark. Sheridan is seated on a filthy pile of straw, dressed in rags. He is bandaging his foot. Pitt approaches, holding a handkerchief over his mouth and nose. He carries a basket.

SHERIDAN. Welcome to debtor's prison, Mister Pitt. Have you come to gloat?

PITT. This is repulsive. A woman just offered me her body and then threw up on my shoes.

SHERIDAN. That'll be Doll Prothroe. Pity the wench, she's not long for this world.

PITT. Could we — could we go indoors? The smell —

SHERIDAN. The gutters here are cleaner than the houses, so I prefer to live *alfresco*. To what do I owe this unexpected pleasure?

PITT. I've brought you some food. I thought you might be hungry. There's a few meat pies, half a roast, a few tankards of ale.

SHERIDAN. *(Clearly starving.)* Ah — no thank you.

PITT. For God's sake, man, take it. You look like death. What's happened to your foot?

SHERIDAN. A gentleman named Slicing Jack cut my shoes off while I slept. Unfortunately, I think he kept a toe into the bargain. Now pronounce your victory and be gone. Enjoy the fruits of my disgrace, but have the decency not to do so to my face. I am trying to maintain some shred of dignity.

65

PITT. And if it's your dignity I'm after?

SHERIDAN. For all your faults, you always spoke your mind. May I return the favor?

PITT. Please.

SHERIDAN. Get stuffed.

PITT. Is that any way to talk to your future benefactor? I have a business proposition for you, Sheridan.

SHERIDAN. Your venture history doesn't recommend you, Pitt. Your last business didn't fare too well.

PITT. Yes, pity about our theatre. My sources tell me it was arson.

SHERIDAN. My sources were convinced that you had done it.

PITT. Me? And why on earth should I? I invested in it.

SHERIDAN. The insurance.

PITT. Ah, now that is clever. I did collect a pretty penny from the deal. I might even be convinced to share it with you. If you accept my offer.

SHERIDAN. I'd rather be a poor man in heaven than reign in hell.

PITT. And what makes you think you'll be allowed in heaven after all the things you've done? Those Frenchmen you supported in your last oration — Danton, Marat, Robespierre — D'you know that every one of them is dead? The bloodbath and the carnage turned upon itself like a wild beast eating its young. If it were up to you, we'd all be following them to their graves.

SHERIDAN. Not all of us: just you.

PITT. Something you've never understood about me, Sheridan: I believe in this country. I don't want to see it torn to shreds. I also believe men like you can be of use — once you're stripped of your illusions. You see, you never were quite one of us. Bloody Irish. Bastard race. True, you may have lived in England all your life, but yet your blood must learn to subjugate itself in order to survive. That is why I have come here today. To offer you a means to save yourself.

SHERIDAN. I may not be the man I was, but yet my virtue can't be had for the price of a pork pie.

PITT. You don't know what I'm offering. I can get you out of here. I can grant your liberty. That is the word you chanted, isn't it — liberty? Now I can outline the proposition and discuss it, or I can leave and you need never see me again.

66

SHERIDAN. Is that the choice you gave Mister Fox?

PITT. For God's sake, man, you have yourself to blame for his demise, now will you quit this game or not? I know what goes on in a place like this. My father was once magistrate of a debtor's prison. You won't last another month. Today it is your toe, tomorrow an arm, and after that your throat gets cut. Do you want to die like that? Oh, what's the use? I should leave you here to rot. Good day.

SHERIDAN. What is it, Mister Pitt?

PITT. *(Pause.)* Here — tuck in while I explain. It'll help you concentrate. *(Pitt places the basket at Sheridan's feet. Sheridan resists touching it.)* There's to be a hearing of the committee in a few days' time. An uncooperative gentleman brought up on a charge of sodomy. I need a witness to secure the verdict on this man. Now I know you disapprove of my dealings in this business, so I appeal instead to your sense of justice.

SHERIDAN. Since when has your committee ever concerned itself with justice?

PITT. Since the gentleman's name is Lord Byron.

SHERIDAN. *(Pause.)* Go on.

PITT. There's not much more to say. I know the man was once your friend. I want to see you ruin him. I want to compromise that sense of loyalty you claim so dear.

SHERIDAN. Tut, Mister Pitt. If I didn't know any better, I'd say you *had* burned my theatre.

PITT. *Our* theatre. And I didn't.

SHERIDAN. Yes, I know. Because I did.

PITT. You? Why, I'll have you locked in Bedlam with the lunatics! Are you mad?

SHERIDAN. *(Laughing.)* Oh, the look on your face has made it worth your visit.

PITT. I shouldn't have come. I shouldn't have even bothered thinking —

SHERIDAN. Mister Pitt — your offer? I accept. *(Pause.)* You get me out of here, get me a proper place to live, and I will tie the noose myself around that traitor's neck.

PITT. *(Offering his hand.)* I'll have your release drawn up at once.

SHERIDAN. I'd rather not touch your hand, Mister Pitt.

PITT. Oh, but I insist. *(Pause. They shake hands.)* There'll be a carriage at the gate to pick you up in half an hour. Have a wash. You smell as though you've passed through the intestines of a dog.

SHERIDAN. Yes, sir.

PITT. Now eat. *(Pause.)* Go on. I want to watch you. *(Sheridan slowly opens the basket and draws out a meat pie. He looks at it.)* It's like a dream, isn't it? After all the progress of this world; all the music, art, philosophy; after all the noble aspirations which have elevated man above a beast, we're left with what? Some chopped-up bits of cow baked in a pastry. That's your humanity. Go on and eat it, man. It's what you're worth. Your price. *(Pause.)* Or do you think it's poisoned? *(Pause. Sheridan takes a bite. Chews. Swallows. Smiling wryly.)* Enjoy your meal. *(Pitt exits. Sheridan tears into the food ravenously.)*

Scene 7

The Old Bailey. Justice McKeye, with ear trumpet, sitting. Pitt stands holding papers. Byron stands before the table in filthy rags. He is bruised. There is a sign of a nosebleed.

PITT. M'lud, with your permission, I would like to rephrase the question so the accused would understand.

McKEYE. Hm? Oh yes. By all means. *(Pitt steps up to Byron and backhands him across the face. Byron falls. Pitt rubs his knuckles.)*

PITT. M'lud, I propose that in future the defendant's plea be arranged prior to the trial date. This sort of business is wasting valuable court time.

BYRON. I will not recognize this as a court of law until I am granted proper council.

McKEYE. Stand up. I can't hear you!

BYRON. I demand proper council!

McKEYE. Lord Byron, this is a simple court. It is concerned with facts. Facts are the truth and the truth is always simple. Now, unless you have something to hide, I would like to proceed.

PITT. What is your plea to the charge made against you?

68

BYRON. Not guilty.

McKEYE. What's that?

PITT. Not guilty!

McKEYE. *(Banging his gavel.)* Not guilty!

PITT. That is his plea, you old fool — not the verdict!

McKEYE. Oh, I see. *(Banging his gavel.)* Order! Order! Silence! *(Pause.)* What now?

PITT. Send for the witness.

McKEYE. What?

PITT. Send for the witness!

McKEYE. *(Banging again.)* Send for the witness! Send for the witness! *(A line of voices is heard offstage calling "Send for the witness!" They grow fainter the farther out they go. Byron rises from the floor. Sheridan enters.)* Are you the witness?

SHERIDAN. Yes, m'lud.

McKEYE. State your name.

SHERIDAN. Richard Brinsley Sheridan.

McKEYE. What is your occupation?

SHERIDAN. Unemployed. My career ended in a blaze of glory. *(Sheridan smiles at Pitt. No reaction.)*

McKEYE. Mister Sheridan, do you swear in the name of God and King George to tell the truth before this committee and bring to light any information requested by it?

SHERIDAN. I do, m'lud.

McKEYE. *(To Pitt.)* Proceed.

PITT. Mister Sheridan, do you recognize the man standing before you?

SHERIDAN. Of course. You are William Pitt, the prime minister.

PITT. The accused. Do you recognize the accused?

SHERIDAN. Yes, I do.

PITT. Would you consider that you know him well?

SHERIDAN. Far too well, unfortunately.

PITT. Mister Sheridan, would you say you are an astute judge of character?

SHERIDAN. Having been a playwright, I would say character is my forte — as opposed to the pianoforte which has never been my métier.

PITT. Answer the question.

SHERIDAN. Yes, I am.

McKEYE. Was there a joke? I —

PITT. Mister Sheridan, the accused, Lord Byron, is charged with moral degeneracy and perversion of character. He is said to be accountable for unnatural practices with members of his own sex. Mister Sheridan, I wonder if you could —

SHERIDAN. May I ask a question?

PITT. Make it short.

SHERIDAN. These "unnatural practices" — were they consensual?

PITT. *(Glaring.)* M'lud, I move that question be stricken from the record.

SHERIDAN. I only ask because, frankly, I wouldn't put him past rape.

PITT. I see. Well, Mister Sheridan, for the moment we are only concerned with establishing the guilt of the accused. We are not interested as of yet with any possible accomplices.

SHERIDAN. Right. Understood.

PITT. Now then. Knowing the accused as you do, could you tell us, has he ever been a married man?

SHERIDAN. No, sir.

PITT. Would you say that he is fond of the company of men?

SHERIDAN. Oh yes.

PITT. Could you be more specific? Does the accused enjoy the company of men in a more — shall we say — rigorous way than yourself?

SHERIDAN. Most decidedly.

McKEYE. Mister Pitt, we are all adults here. If you are trying to say the accused is a shirt-lifter, I wish you'd get on with it. We are rather pressed for time.

PITT. Mister Sheridan, the court wishes to know if you are aware that the accused, Lord Byron, is a practicing sodomite.

SHERIDAN. Lord Byron is far too arrogant a man to practice anything. He'd need to get it right the first time round. *(Justice McKeye can't resist a slight giggle.)*

PITT. Mister Sheridan, do you understand what perversion means?

SHERIDAN. I think so.

PITT. Do you comprehend the serious nature of this committee's brief?

SHERIDAN. I do.

PITT. Why have you chosen to come forward and appear as a witness for this court?

SHERIDAN. I have chosen to come forward and appear as a witness for this court because I believe in the principles and ideals which have made this country an example to the world of decency, humanity, and integrity.

PITT. Thank you.

McKEYE. Very nicely put.

SHERIDAN. And because you paid me.

PITT. Strike that answer!

McKEYE. *(Straining to hear.)* What? What was that? Say again?

PITT. I would like to ask one final question, Mister Sheridan. And I beg you to consider the gravity of these proceedings. As you are this great upholder of the ideals and principles of decency, would you say that the accused, Lord Byron, is lacking in these qualities? That he is an example of corruption and moral degeneracy?

SHERIDAN. *(Looks at Byron. Pause.)* Yes — and no.

PITT. It's either one or the other, Mister Sheridan. Which is it?

SHERIDAN. Well, it's all rather relative, don't you think?

PITT. Just answer the question.

SHERIDAN. — If, for example, you compare him to the Holy Virgin, then yes, I would say he is a thorough degenerate worthy of hanging —

PITT. Thank you. That is all.

SHERIDAN. — But if, on the other hand, you compared him to me —

PITT. That is all!

McKEYE. What did he say?

SHERIDAN. — Or better yet, you, Mister Pitt —

PITT. That is all!

SHERIDAN. — I'd say the angel Gabriel could not improve on the man.

McKEYE. Dammit, what's he saying?

SHERIDAN. *(To McKeye; loud.)* He is not!

PITT. One moment, m'lud, if I may —

McKEYE. Thank you, Mister Sheridan.

PITT. M'lud, I am not satisfied with this witness.

71

McKEYE. What?

PITT. I am not satisfied with this witness!

McKEYE. He seems pleasant enough to me. Lord Byron — *(McKeye picks up the gavel. Pitt grabs it.)*

PITT. Damn your ears — give me that!

McKEYE. *(Grabbing back the gavel; affronted:)* I beg your pardon, Mister Pitt! You brought this witness before the court and he has been fully compliant. Lord Byron, the authority of this committee has found no evidence to support its claim. You are free to go. *(McKeye bangs the gavel.)*

PITT. Authority? I am the authority of this committee!

BYRON. Thank you, m'lud.

PITT. I am not satisfied!

McKEYE. Come, come, Mister Pitt. We've got three other cases today and I know you don't like to be late.

PITT. You bloody incompetent fool!

McKEYE. Thank you for your cooperation, Mister Sheridan.

SHERIDAN. I wonder, m'lud, may I ask one final question?

McKEYE. By all means.

SHERIDAN. Mister Pitt — are you a married man? *(Pitt lunges at Sheridan, choking him. They fall to the floor and struggle. Justice McKeye bangs his gavel furiously.)*

McKEYE. Order! Order! Mister Pitt, this is an outrage! Control yourself, man! *(Sheridan shoves Pitt away. They stand. Pitt swings around and, with an animalistic howl, overturns the table, sending papers flying. Pitt exits. McKeye exits after him, running.)* Mister Pitt! Mister Pitt! *(Silence. Sheridan straightens his clothes and brushes himself off. Byron stands watching him. Sheridan does not look at him.)*

BYRON. Thank you. *(Pause.)* It's not just boys, you know. I could love anything if it let me.

SHERIDAN. I've always held that nothing is unnatural that is not physically impossible.

BYRON. *(Pause.)* Why did you do it?

SHERIDAN. For a man who's always talking about actions and ideals, you don't understand them very well. *(Pause. Looking at Byron.)* I suppose I wanted to do one right thing for the right reasons. I wanted to remember what that feels like. It may be an old man's nature to forget, but it is an old man's duty to forgive.

BYRON. And a young man? What is he to do?

SHERIDAN. Prepare himself.

BYRON. *(Pause.)* Can I — can I buy you a drink?

SHERIDAN. No. I don't think so. *(Sheridan looks away. Silence.)*

BYRON. What will you do now?

SHERIDAN. Get sent back to debtor's prison, I shouldn't wonder. After that, bugger only knows. No offense. And — you?

BYRON. I've been thinking of travel. Rome, or possibly Greece. For a longer stay. This country holds no interest for me anymore.

SHERIDAN. You must — *(Long pause.)* You must send me your next poem — when you've written it. I'd like to read it.

BYRON. I will.

SHERIDAN. Make it funny. Life's too full of darkness. One good laugh is worth a million tears. *(Byron stares at Sheridan. Sheridan stares at the floor. Silence.)* Right — well — I'll be off. Best of luck to you, George.

BYRON. And to you. *(With a vague wave of his hand, Sheridan turns to go.)* Come with me, Richard. Greece is beautiful this time of year. The Acropolis at dawn is something from a dream. *(Sheridan smiles. He takes Byron's face in his hands and kisses him on the forehead. He releases him and steps away. There are tears in his eyes.)*

SHERIDAN. I can't stand classical ruins. Too much like looking in a mirror. *(Sheridan smiles and pats Byron on the cheek. He turns and exits, whistling to himself, kicking papers as he goes. Byron turns and looks out at the sun which, for a moment, gets brighter.)*

End of Play

73

PROPERTY LIST

Drinks
Letter
Props (HOPKINS)
Bottle (SHERIDAN)
Woman's undergarment (SHERIDAN, HOPKINS)
Plate of chicken (POPE)
Mirror (POPE)
Makeup (POPE, PERDITA)
Red wig (HOPKINS)
Newspaper (PERDITA)
Knife (PERDITA)
Handkerchief (BYRON, PITT)
Tablecloth (SHERIDAN)
Sausage (PERDITA)
Hat (PERDITA)
Wooden walking stick (FOX)
Clothes, wig, etc. (SERVANTS)
Damp cloth (GEORGE III)
Silver-tipped walking stick (FOX)
Pouch of money (PITT, SHERIDAN)
Carrot (GEORGE III)
Bottle of wine (SHERIDAN, RAMMAGE)
Candles (DEVONSHIRE)
Stack of scripts (HOPKINS)
Prop crown (HOPKINS)
Playing cards (SHERIDAN)
Paper, ink and pen (HOPKINS, DEVONSHIRE)
Dress case (PERDITA)
Dresses (PERDITA)
Drinking glasses (BYRON)
Gavel (McKEYE)
Ear trumpet (McKEYE)
Papers (PITT)
Pen (PITT)
Book (PITT)
Carafe of wine and glass (SHERIDAN)
Bandage (SHERIDAN)
Basket containing a meat pie (PITT)

SOUND EFFECTS

Stringed instruments mixed with the chatter of women
    and fluttering of fans
Music
Voice-overs
Sound of shattering glass
Horseshoes on pavement
Rumble of voices
Gavel
Cries of assent and approval
Laughter
Roar of voices and stamping feet
Cries of "liberty!"
Thunderstorm
Hoofbeats
Rain
Bell
Fire
Woman humming lullaby
Dogs barking

NEW PLAYS

★ **HONOUR by Joanna Murray-Smith.** In a series of intense confrontations, a wife, husband, lover and daughter negotiate the forces of passion, history, responsibility and honour. "HONOUR makes for surprisingly interesting viewing. Tight, crackling dialogue (usually played out in punchy verbal duels) captures characters unable to deal with emotions ... Murray-Smith effectively places her characters in situations that strip away pretense." *–Variety* "... the play's virtues are strong: a distinctive theatrical voice, passionate concerns ... HONOUR might just capture a few honors of its own." *–Time Out Magazine* [1M, 3W] ISBN: 0-8222-1683-3

★ **MR. PETERS' CONNECTIONS by Arthur Miller.** Mr. Miller describes the protagonist as existing in a dream-like state when the mind is "freed to roam from real memories to conjectures, from trivialities to tragic insights, from terror of death to glorying in one's being alive." With this memory play, the Tony Award and Pulitzer Prize-winner reaffirms his stature as the world's foremost dramatist. "... a cross between Joycean stream-of-consciousness and Strindberg's dream plays, sweetened with a dose of William Saroyan's philosophical whimsy ... CONNECTIONS is most intriguing ..." *–The NY Times* [5M, 3W] ISBN: 0-8222-1687-6

★ **THE WAITING ROOM by Lisa Loomer.** Three women from different centuries meet in a doctor's waiting room in this dark comedy about the timeless quest for beauty – and its cost. "... THE WAITING ROOM ... is a bold, risky melange of conflicting elements that is ... terrifically moving ... There's no resisting the fierce emotional pull of the play." *–The NY Times* "... one of the high points of this year's Off-Broadway season ... THE WAITING ROOM is well worth a visit." *–Back Stage* [7M, 4W, flexible casting] ISBN: 0-8222-1594-2

★ **THE OLD SETTLER by John Henry Redwood.** A sweet-natured comedy about two church-going sisters in 1943 Harlem and the handsome young man who rents a room in their apartment. "For all of its decent sentiments, THE OLD SETTLER avoids sentimentality. It has the authenticity and lack of pretense of an Early American sampler." *–The NY Times* "We've had some fine plays Off-Broadway this season, and this is one of the best." *–The NY Post* [1M, 3W] ISBN: 0-8-222-1642-6

★ **LAST TRAIN TO NIBROC by Arlene Hutton.** In 1940 two young strangers share a seat on a train bound east only to find their paths will cross again. "All aboard. LAST TRAIN TO NIBROC is a sweetly told little chamber romance." *–Show Business* "... [a] gently charming little play, reminiscent of Thornton Wilder in its look at rustic Americans who are to be treasured for their simplicity and directness ..." *–Associated Press* "The old formula of boy wins girls, boy loses girl, boy wins girl still works ... [a] well-made play that perfectly captures a slice of small-town-life-gone-by." *–Back Stage* [1M, 1W] ISBN: 0-8222-1753-8

★ **OVER THE RIVER AND THROUGH THE WOODS by Joe DiPietro.** Nick sees both sets of his grandparents every Sunday for dinner. This is routine until he has to tell them that he's been offered a dream job in Seattle. The news doesn't sit so well. "A hilarious family comedy that is even funnier than his long running musical revue *I Love You, You're Perfect, Now Change.*" *–Back Stage* "Loaded with laughs every step of the way." *–Star-Ledger* [3M, 3W] ISBN: 0-8222-1712-0

★ **SIDE MAN by Warren Leight.** 1999 Tony Award winner. This is the story of a broken family and the decline of jazz as popular entertainment. "... a tender, deeply personal memory play about the turmoil in the family of a jazz musician as his career crumbles at the dawn of the age of rock-and-roll ..." *–The NY Times* "[SIDE MAN] is an elegy for two things – a lost world and a lost love. When the two notes sound together in harmony, it is moving and graceful ..." *–The NY Daily News* "An atmospheric memory play ... with crisp dialogue and clearly drawn characters ... reflects the passing of an era with persuasive insight ... The joy and despair of the musicians is skillfully illustrated." *–Variety* [5M, 3W] ISBN: 0-8222-1721-X

DRAMATISTS PLAY SERVICE, INC.
440 Park Avenue South, New York, NY 10016 212-683-8960 Fax 212-213-1539
postmaster@dramatists.com   www.dramatists.com

NEW PLAYS

★ **CLOSER by Patrick Marber.** Winner of the 1998 Olivier Award for Best Play and the 1999 New York Drama Critics Circle Award for Best Foreign Play. Four lives intertwine over the course of four and a half years in this densely plotted, stinging look at modern love and betrayal. "CLOSER is a sad, savvy, often funny play that casts a steely, unblinking gaze at the world of relationships and lets you come to your own conclusions ... CLOSER does not merely hold your attention; it burrows into you." *–New York Magazine* "A powerful, darkly funny play about the cosmic collision between the sun of love and the comet of desire." *–Newsweek Magazine* [2M, 2W] ISBN: 0-8222-1722-8

★ **THE MOST FABULOUS STORY EVER TOLD by Paul Rudnick.** A stage manager, headset and prompt book at hand, brings the house lights to half, then dark, and cues the creation of the world. Throughout the play, she's in control of everything. In other words, she's either God, or she thinks she is. "Line by line, Mr. Rudnick may be the funniest writer for the stage in the United States today ... One-liners, epigrams, withering put-downs and flashing repartee: These are the candles that Mr. Rudnick lights instead of cursing the darkness ... a testament to the virtues of laughing ... and in laughter, there is something like the memory of Eden." *–The NY Times* "Funny it is ... consistently, rapaciously, deliriously ... easily the funniest play in town." *–Variety* [4M, 5W] ISBN: 0-8222-1720-1

★ **A DOLL'S HOUSE by Henrik Ibsen, adapted by Frank McGuinness.** Winner of the 1997 Tony Award for Best Revival. "New, raw, gut-twisting and gripping. Easily the hottest drama this season." *–USA Today* "Bold, brilliant and alive." *–The Wall Street Journal* "A thunderclap of an evening that takes your breath away." *–Time Magazine* [4M, 4W, 2 boys] ISBN: 0-8222-1636-1

★ **THE HERBAL BED by Peter Whelan.** The play is based on actual events which occurred in Stratford-upon-Avon in the summer of 1613, when William Shakespeare's elder daughter was publicly accused of having a sexual liaison with a married neighbor and family friend. "In his probing new play, THE HERBAL BED ... Peter Whelan muses about a sidelong event in the life of Shakespeare's family and creates a finely textured tapestry of love and lies in the early 17th-century Stratford." *–The NY Times* "It is a first rate drama with interesting moral issues of truth and expediency." *–The NY Post* [5M, 3W] ISBN: 0-8222-1675-2

★ **SNAKEBIT by David Marshall Grant.** A study of modern friendship when put to the test. "... a rather smart and absorbing evening of water-cooler theater, the intimate sort of Off-Broadway experience that has you picking apart the recognizable characters long after the curtain calls." *–The NY Times* "Off-Broadway keeps on presenting us with compelling reasons for going to the theater. The latest is SNAKEBIT, David Marshall Grant's smart new comic drama about being thirtysomething and losing one's way in life." *–The NY Daily News* [3M, 1W] ISBN: 0-8222-1724-4

★ **A QUESTION OF MERCY by David Rabe.** The Obie Award-winning playwright probes the sensitive and controversial issue of doctor-assisted suicide in the age of AIDS in this poignant drama. "There are many devastating ironies in Mr. Rabe's beautifully considered, piercingly clear-eyed work ..." *–The NY Times* "With unsettling candor and disturbing insight, the play arouses pity and understanding of a troubling subject ... Rabe's provocative tale is an affirmation of dignity that rings clear and true." *–Variety* [6M, 1W] ISBN: 0-8222-1643-4

★ **DIMLY PERCEIVED THREATS TO THE SYSTEM by Jon Klein.** Reality and fantasy overlap with hilarious results as this unforgettable family attempts to survive the nineties. "Here's a play whose point about fractured families goes to the heart, mind – and ears." *–The Washington Post* "... an end-of-the millennium comedy about a family on the verge of a nervous breakdown ... Trenchant and hilarious ..." *–The Baltimore Sun* [2M, 4W] ISBN: 0-8222-1677-9

DRAMATISTS PLAY SERVICE, INC.
440 Park Avenue South, New York, NY 10016 212-683-8960 Fax 212-213-1539
postmaster@dramatists.com   www.dramatists.com

NEW PLAYS

★ **AS BEES IN HONEY DROWN by Douglas Carter Beane.** Winner of the John Gassner Playwriting Award. A hot young novelist finds the subject of his new screenplay in a New York socialite who leads him into the world of *Auntie Mame* and *Breakfast at Tiffany's*, before she takes him for a ride. "A delicious soufflé of a satire ... [an] extremely entertaining fable for an age that always chooses image over substance." *—The NY Times* "... A witty assessment of one of the most active and relentless industries in a consumer society ... the creation of 'hot' young things, which the media have learned to mass produce with efficiency and zeal." *—The NY Daily News* [3M, 3W, flexible casting] ISBN: 0-8222-1651-5

★ **STUPID KIDS by John C. Russell.** In rapid, highly stylized scenes, the story follows four high-school students as they make their way from first through eighth period and beyond, struggling with the fears, frustrations, and longings peculiar to youth. "In STUPID KIDS ... playwright John C. Russell gets the opera of adolescence to a T ... The stylized teenspeak of STUPID KIDS ... suggests that Mr. Russell may have hidden a tape recorder under a desk in study hall somewhere and then scoured the tapes for good quotations ... it is the kids' insular, ceaselessly churning world, a pre-adult world of Doritos and libidos, that the playwright seeks to lay bare." *—The NY Times* "STUPID KIDS [is] a sharp-edged ... whoosh of teen angst and conformity anguish. It is also very funny." *—NY Newsday* [2M, 2W] ISBN: 0-8222-1698-1

★ **COLLECTED STORIES by Donald Margulies.** From Obie Award-winner Donald Margulies comes a provocative analysis of a student-teacher relationship that turns sour when the protégé becomes a rival. "With his fine ear for detail, Margulies creates an authentic, insular world, and he gives equal weight to the opposing viewpoints of two formidable characters." *—The LA Times* "This is probably Margulies' best play to date ..." *—The NY Post* "... always fluid and lively, the play is thick with ideas, like a stock-pot of good stew." *—The Village Voice* [2W] ISBN: 0-8222-1640-X

★ **FREEDOMLAND by Amy Freed.** An overdue showdown between a son and his father sets off fireworks that illuminate the neurosis, rage and anxiety of one family – and of America at the turn of the millennium. "FREEDOMLAND's more obvious links are to *Buried Child* and *Bosoms and Neglect*. Freed, like Guare, is an inspired wordsmith with a gift for surreal touches in situations grounded in familiar and real territory." *—Curtain Up* [3M, 4W] ISBN: 0-8222-1719-8

★ **STOP KISS by Diana Son.** A poignant and funny play about the ways, both sudden and slow, that lives can change irrevocably. "There's so much that is vital and exciting about STOP KISS ... you want to embrace this young author and cheer her onto other works ... the writing on display here is funny and credible ... you also will be charmed by its heartfelt characters and up-to-the-minute humor." *—The NY Daily News* "... irresistibly exciting ... a sweet, sad, and enchantingly sincere play." *—The NY Times* [3M, 3W] ISBN: 0-8222-1731-7

★ **THREE DAYS OF RAIN by Richard Greenberg.** The sins of fathers and mothers make for a bittersweet elegy in this poignant and revealing drama. "... a work so perfectly judged it heralds the arrival of a major playwright ... Greenberg is extraordinary." *—The NY Daily News* "Greenberg's play is filled with graceful passages that are by turns melancholy, harrowing, and often, quite funny." *—Variety* [2M, 1W] ISBN: 0-8222-1676-0

★ **THE WEIR by Conor McPherson.** In a bar in rural Ireland, the local men swap spooky stories in an attempt to impress a young woman from Dublin who recently moved into a nearby "haunted" house. However, the tables are soon turned when she spins a yarn of her own. "You shed all sense of time at this beautiful and devious new play." *—The NY Times* "Sheer theatrical magic. I have rarely been so convinced that I have just seen a modern classic. Tremendous." *—The London Daily Telegraph* [4M, 1W] ISBN: 0-8222-1706-6

DRAMATISTS PLAY SERVICE, INC.
440 Park Avenue South, New York, NY 10016 212-683-8960 Fax 212-213-1539
postmaster@dramatists.com   www.dramatists.com